*un*WORTHY
BUT
WELCOME

A GUIDE FOR STARTING OVERCOMERS AND SERENITY CHURCH

Serenity
Power for the Powerless

and

RIGHT LINE PUBLISHING

*un*WORTHY
BUT
WELCOME

Besides, worthy was never the point!

A GUIDE FOR STARTING OVERCOMERS AND SERENITY CHURCH

Heart and Mind-Changing Testimonies

from

Serenity Church
The Colony, Texas

a companion to *Never Alone Again*
by John Featherston

Compiled by
Linda Widhalm

Isa 58:6-10

Serenity Church of Dallas
P. O. Box 560487
The Colony, TX 75056

http://www.serenitychurch.net

Serenity Church of Dallas, Texas, located in Dallas's northern suburb of The Colony, was formed in 2006 to bring worship and recovery together in one place.

Serenity Church of Dallas partners with Metro Relief in The Colony and with Sunlight Missionary Baptist Church in Dallas to bring Serenity Church worship services, Overcomers groups, food, clothing, and other assistance to folks in the Cooper Street neighborhood of South Dallas. Many other groups and individuals from around the Dallas/Ft. Worth Metroplex also join us to bring Christ's love and light to the struggling people living in the South Dallas area.

ISBN-13: 978-0-9844395-7-7
ISBN-10: 0-9844395-7-9

REL014000 RELIGION / Christian Church / Administration
REL012020 RELIGION / Christian Life / Devotional
SEL032000 SELF-HELP / Spiritual
SEL026000 SELF-HELP / Substance Abuse & Addictions / General

Published by
Right Line Publishing, New Richmond, Wisconsin

Printed in the U.S.A.

Dedicated
to Jesus Christ

for the furtherance of His Kingdom on earth
in the hearts of folks like us
so that others will come to understand
like Lael did:

"I came here and figured out that,
yeah, you're unworthy, but you're still welcome!"

and, as David reminded us,

"that no one misses the grace of God."

Compiler's Note

This book was accomplished with the help of many individuals who are named along the way, and was inspired by many others.

My sincere thanks to everyone with a by-line for your humble honesty and dedication to our Higher Power, Jesus Christ, as evidenced by your working of the 12th Step through contributing to *Unworthy but Welcome*: *A Guide for Starting Overcomers and Serenity Church.*

The advice we offer to anyone feeling led to begin a Christ-based ministry in the recovery community is to first read *Never Alone Again* by John Featherston then read how we do Overcomers and Serenity Church by reading this book, *Unworthy but Welcome*, front to back. Also visit our website, www.serenitychurch.net, and listen to some recovery sermons. At whatever points you may be offended by what you read or hear, pause and ask the Holy Spirit to guide you. We must overcome our own judgements and offenses to minister the love and healing of Jesus Christ to hurting, broken people.

This is our prayer. Jesus is Lord.

Linda

Contents

Foreword

On Friday, March 13th, I found myself out of a job. It was a job I hated with a company I had increasing moral concerns about, but it had been a steady paycheck for several years. That Saturday I woke up and the panic set in. I began taking inventory of my spiritual support network and found it to be lacking — in fact, in the year prior to that it had essentially been gutted and ripped out of my life. I prayed that morning that God would bring me to a group of healthy, thriving believers where I could continue to not only grow but question my faith.

One week later I walked through the doors of Serenity Church for the very first time. As the service went on I noticed puffs of vapor rose from the congregation, the bass player was showing more ink than my theology text books, and then this guy got up to preach and he wasn't wearing any shoes! In my own head, I looked up to God and said, "Really? Perhaps I should have been more specific!"

But as I experienced the Sereni-liturgy for the first time, and sat in a circle for an Overcomers meeting for the first time, I knew beyond a shadow of a doubt that I was home.

If this is your first time with us, brace yourself — we are so glad you are here, and I hope and pray you experience the same answered prayers that I have: that we would all find great peace in being one with God and His people.

Laura Beth

Preface

I was sitting in the pews that first Saturday night, June 4th, 2006, when everything I heard seemed to match the longing in my heart. Not that I understood everything I was hearing—so I asked God to bring understanding. Not that my pristine ivory tower was not offended—so I asked Him to keep tearing it down. After all, He's the one who put the longing in my heart.

What did I hear? Raw honesty expressed by folks who had been to the pit—the depths of sin, despair, loneliness, isolation, financial ruin, and every other desperation brought about by sin, addiction, depression, and grief. But these folks held their heads high, eyes and hearts aglow with joy, as they uttered every word. These folks were real.

I was so weary of the struggle of trying to worship with folks hiding behind ivory tower masks. After all, I had a mask of my own! Many masks, in fact. I discovered that although I could be real with God inwardly, most people I worshiped with did not want to know about it. Now, here at last, was a place where it was okay to get rid of every mask because we shouldn't have to wear a mask when we know God is pleased with us. Here was a place I could get comfortable being me. A place where I could be real with real people. They were already teaching me how.

Lael said,

"I'm broken and weak. But He still wants me...

and He wants me to follow Him."

Come on in! We believe God brought you here for a reason. Welcome! We're glad you came!

Introduction

What is Serenity Church?

Serenity Church is a place where broken people find healing. A place for those suffering hurts beyond their control, for whom life has become unmanageable, and who have no idea what to do next. It is a place where the lonely find a home, the hopeless find hope, the hurting find healing, the outcast is welcomed, the powerless find power, and the broken have the pieces put back together.

Serenity Church welcomes those with tattoos, body piercings, and long hair—as well as those who don't. We welcome those who come by car or bicycle, on foot or motorcycle. We welcome those wearing shorts and flip flops, leather and studs, ball caps and cowboy hats, suits and dresses, clean clothes and dirty. Whatever our personal preferences are we keep them to ourselves and ask God to give us welcoming smiles and hugs for everyone. Rarely does someone come who won't receive a hug—at least by their second visit.

Serenity Church is a place that is reaching out with the restoring power of God to people who are sick and tired of being sick and tired.

Serenity Church, from the ground up, at its core, is a recovery church. It was born out of Overcomers, and our goal is that once someone steps through the doors of Serenity Church they will begin to know:

> These people are glad I'm here!
> I never have to be alone in my struggles again.
> These people know what I'm going through—they've been there.
> My coming here was no accident!

This testimony came by e-mail in 2008:

> "You have welcomed me and my family during a hurting time. It has been incredible to be among people who genuinely care about the person and not the status. I listen to all of you give your testimonies and I am just amazed at the things God is doing in all of our lives. I brought you my broken family and you loved us and that is awesome!!!!! I have had the tremendous opportunity to help families, build churches, and save lives. I have led many people

to Christ all over the place. A lot of them call me from different states and it's just a blessing that God lets me be the vessel. I have empowered women to do great things, but when I was falling apart and I was losing my own child and watching my ex-husband destroy his life, I found a place where it was okay to cry. It was okay to bring my ex-husband and be married to my current husband. I was not judged, I did not have to be fancy, I did not have to be the rock. God brought me to your door and you let me in, and I am so very grateful as I watch my child who was going down the wrong path now excited and even learning to play the guitar [at Serenity Church]! I watch my ex-husband getting better and walking sober day by day. Getting closer to our Lord. I see things in myself that I can change and be better one day at a time. I truly love you all and I thank you for loving me and my family.

– Sherry Menefee

We believe God brings everyone who comes for a purpose. It may be to begin a journey of recovery. It may be to give their Higher Power a name: Jesus Christ. Maybe they need a place to worship where they and their family are all welcome. It may be to have a safe place to bring a struggling friend. In every case, we consider God to be answering our prayer in giving us what we're missing.

We're so glad when people get what they're missing, too! We found that we can lay aside our differences to sit in recovery circles together, so there is no reason we should not be able to do the same as we worship the same Higher Power together. We have discovered that what we have in common is far greater than what we have that is different.

St. Augustine said, "In essentials, unity; in non-essentials, liberty; in all things, charity." Many of us have not been comfortable in neat and tidy churches. Many of us have not been welcomed there. Some of us have been chased out the door or asked not to come back; but as Pastor John said to me one day, "I can't imagine Jesus standing in the aisle of any church telling someone they weren't welcome there." So we believe we must not only let everyone in who wants to come, but we must welcome them with open arms as Jesus would.

Adrian Rogers said, "Jesus doesn't change us so He can love us, He loves us so He can change us." Well, we think Jesus just loves us. If change were the aim, then His love would be conditional. His aim is love. Change is a byproduct. When we are exposed to His love through each other, we do begin to change.

First, we begin to change our minds about being loveable. Other good stuff follows. At Serenity Church we try to focus on loving one another as Jesus told us to do. He said if we are loving each other, we are loving Him.

*T*hen the righteous will answer Him, "Lord, when did we see You hungry, and feed You, or thirsty, and give You something to drink? And when did we see You a stranger, and invite You in, or naked, and clothe You? When did we see You sick, or in prison, and come to You?"

The King will answer and say to them, "Truly I say to you, to the extent that you did it to one of these brothers of Mine, even the least of them, you did it to Me" (Matthew 25:37-40).

This book has been compiled for you—the one who is seeking to know, even more, the mind, heart, and will of God; the one who has been wounded and tends to run away from church; anyone who has chosen to accept the free gift of God through Jesus Christ; anyone struggling to hold on to sobriety, sanity, or life; anyone begging God for sobriety for a loved one; anyone who has heard of Serenity Church and wants to know how to start one where they live. This book is to help make you ready.

Seven years after Sherry Menefee brought her hurting, broken family to Serenity Church she reports:

My ex-husband is still sober, one son is in college and working, my other son is in the Air Force, so I am very thankful for my time at Serenity.

Section 1

HOLY COMMUNION

"Jesus Christ, Himself,
preserves the sanctity of that table."

– Aunt Laurie

Introduction to Holy Communion

Holy Communion
The Lord's Table
The Lord's Supper
The Eucharist
The Great Thanksgiving

Different names but each is the same reverent celebration of God's provision for the forgiveness of sins through the sacrifice of Jesus Christ by sharing together the bread, representing the body of Jesus that was broken for us, and the juice, representing His blood which was shed for us.

The table which Jesus set before us to do in remembrance of Him, to bring us into fellowship with Him and with one another, is the very place many have felt excluded, out of fellowship with Him and one another and, therefore, not holding fond remembrances of Him and His followers.

At Serenity Church all are welcome to partake of the Lord's Table. All are welcomed first by an invitation that can be read in the bulletin, then by the person overseeing communion, and again by someone bringing a communion meditation.

The following pages hold many examples and testimonies. Read them all. Ponder them all. In the places where you are offended or challenged, ask the Holy Spirit for help. It is not our intention to harm, cast blame, or be disrespectful. It is our aim to celebrate with great thanksgiving the high price He paid for our salvation and to bring many to repentance.

Communion Sharing

Communion Sharing is about three minutes of sharing from your heart about what Communion means to you; with this, you "open the doors to the dining room" for your family. It does not have to be a dramatic presentation with props—although we have been blessed with some of those. A simple message coming from the heart can be as captivating and meaningful as something dramatic. Typing it out and reading it can ease nervousness, help keep to the time limit, and help you not leave anything out.

The beauty of Serenity Church is we have a wonderful variety of people here and we would like to hear from everyone. If you have never done a Communion Sharing, or if it's been a long time, please volunteer.

– Aunt Laurie Gorrell

Serenity Church Prayer
by John Featherston

Jesus is Lord. Jesus is Lord. Jesus is Lord.
Jesus is Lord. Jesus is Lord.
Father, please show us what we're missing.
Father, please give us what we're missing.
Heal our minds, our hearts and our bodies—through Christ.
This is our prayer: Jesus is Lord.

—our prayer for you as you read and ponder.

Communion Sharing from the Heart

CLEAR THE TABLE
Linda Widhalm, October 2009

When I was a child this table was not approachable by me. Only men gathered around it and then carefully shared it with a select group of people. I was not one of them. Eventually I came to understand there was a list of pre-requisites for me to be able to take part in this very special, sacred ritual, and a whole other list to be able to keep on taking it. But Jesus said, "... do this in remembrance of Me" (Luke 22:19). He said it to His disciples.

A few weeks ago, David Roberts shared from Scripture all the benefits we have from the death of Jesus. All those benefits are only needed by needy people. Jesus, Himself, said, "It is not the healthy who need a doctor, but the sick" (Luke 5:31).

At Serenity Church we don't have any pre-requisites for taking communion. The following story really helped me "clear the table" of everything that would hinder my coming to His table. It was written by Rev. Dr. Gail Ricciuti.

She writes:

> Anthony and I began the relationship with Farley, our Sheltie, according to strict rules. No table scraps! No begging at meals! Before dinner was ready each evening he would take his place under the table where my feet would go. A good place from which to grab any crumb that might fall!

> As time went by, the table rules got bent a little more. He was so much a part of us, more and more not a foreign breed. He understood our speech and we came to understand his much fuller vocabulary of whimper, posture, body language, claw, touch, nudge, stare, ear twitch. And so, at breakfast each morning, Farley eventually got a bit of toast (one of his favorite things) and at the end of dinner, a choice bit of meat or fish, saved for him from my plate. If I lingered too long before offering it, I'd notice a chin delicately laid on my knee—just a reminder.

He lived heartily for eight years, and then suddenly, cancer—before he had ever come near old age. Months later, when he lost his appetite for the dog food he had always relished, the rules became irrelevant. Mealtime became an inventory of the refrigerator. Whatever he would eat, he could have: tuna, yogurt, steak, cottage cheese. When he became too tired to bend and eat from his dish on the floor, then he got it from my hand. Last, he got premium baby food—strained meat—fed a teaspoon at a time from a syringe.

Missing him as we do, I look back now and realize what happened: gradually he changed my mind about the artificial demarcation that we call "species." He changed my mind about "table rules," ... about ritual purity. I found myself letting go of all our rules, all our contrived distinctions; knowing that what was important was not that he be differentiated from us like some lesser creature; but that the life he had be nourished. Farley's lovely life had changed me; I'd have lifted him up onto the table if only it had meant that he could eat.

And so here we are. I believe the heart of Jesus is that you be nourished; that nothing and no one hinder you from coming to get what you need. I pray this story has helped you "clear the table" of everything that would keep you from coming tonight to His table.

Some of you here tonight have friends and relatives who feel just as this woman did. They have been agonizing over your condition. If you would just eat—they would do whatever it takes for you to get what you need so that you can go on living and not dying. The thing is, someone else already did exactly what it takes for you to get everything you need to live and not die. His name is Jesus. This table is a good place to come to meet Him.

By Virtue of an Invitation
Aunt Laurie, August 2010

A few weeks ago I went to a Sunday morning church where they were serving the Lord's Supper. Before partaking, the pastor read from 1 Corinthians 11:27-29:

> "Wherefore, whosoever shall eat this bread, and drink this cup of the Lord, unworthily, shall be guilty of the body and blood of the Lord. But let a man examine himself, and so let him eat of that bread, and drink of that cup. For he that eateth and drinketh unworthily, eateth and drinketh judgment to himself, not discerning the Lord's body" (KJV).

A checklist was provided in the bulletin so each worshiper could make sure they are worthy to participate.

1. Be Baptized in the name of the Father, Son, and Holy Spirit

2. Be a member of a Christ-centered church

3. Give 10% of your income to your local church

4. Live an orderly and correct life

And so on, for a total of ten questions.

I was feeling rather smug about my performance on the checklist when I stopped and asked myself, "What am I doing?!?!?" Accomplishing these ideals is not what makes me worthy to come to this table. I'm worthy by virtue of an invitation. If I could conduct myself consistently like *that* I wouldn't need to come to this table or to embrace what this table is supposed to help me remember.

I come to this table worthily, not because I've earned it through my own efforts, but because I remember why I'm here and what it cost to invite me. I'm worthy because I humbly and gratefully remember Him.

We really miss the point sometimes.

Communion as the 12ᵀᴴ Step
Linda Widhalm, 2007

Hello! My name is Linda and I'm an Overcomer. I became an official Overcomer on Saturday, September 2, 2006. I will never forget the Saturday before that date. It was August 26. Serenity Church was completing the first round of preaching through the 12 Steps. Step 12 says, "Having had a spiritual awakening as a result of these Steps, we tried to carry the message to others and practice these principles in all our affairs." To practice this Step, during communion we were invited to take communion on behalf of another person who needed Jesus. Immediately, my heart was stirred for the person I'd take communion for. I began praying for that person as I waited in line, as I took the bread, as I dipped it in the cup. Then I spoke that name before eating.

Seven days later my phone rang and that person was on the other end of the line asking for help. Six hours later they were sitting beside me here at Serenity Church. Two hours after that they entered with me, for the first time for both of us, through the doors and into the circle of Overcomers.

I have to say that a *lot* has changed in my life since that day. Some of the change has been in my heart, but most of it has been in my head. When my heart is stirred for the needs of another, my head reminds my heart that Jesus is the answer to everything, not me or anything I can do, just Jesus. Yes, sometimes He guides me to love other people by helping or praying for them, but lasting *help* is something that can only happen between them and Jesus.

For me, each time I take communion it is an opportunity to remind myself that *all* I need is found in Jesus. Tonight maybe there is something you need that you haven't fully relied on Jesus for. Let me encourage you to "Speak it out" when you eat. It may be for healing: "Lord, heal my back." It may regard a job: "Lord, shine Your favor upon me at my next job interview." It may simply be a desire for His presence: "Lord, I need *You*—to fill my loneliness, to lift my spirit, to comfort me." Or you may need to practice the 12ᵗʰ Step by praying for Light to dawn in the heart of a loved one. If so, speak their name out before you eat.

Plans
Pat Widhalm, 2008

Hi, I'm Pat. I'm an Overcomer. I'm a planner, and I like things when they go according to plan. I strongly suspect all of you are pretty much the same. It's a good thing. That's the way that God designed us—you can't be the custodian of the world (no matter how bad a job we are doing) if you can't create and execute a sound plan. You are here tonight because you planned to be here, and you know what is happening because the plan is laid out for you in the bulletin. We like to be in control, and a good plan gives us the illusion that we are.

When I was a much younger man, my younger brother, Bob, gave me this Bible. It is *The Living Bible*, a paraphrase version. There aren't any Thees or Thous, Begats, Begottens, B'Goshes, or B'Gollies. It puts the message in easy to understand plain English. At the time I wasn't doing much Bible reading, but this Bible was the first one I read that spoke to my heart. It came alive for me and I ate it up. I read it cover to cover and, to this day, much of what I remember in the Bible is based on what I read in this version.

One of my favorite verses is Proverbs 19:21. It talks about a man's plans and very succinctly puts it: "Man proposes, but God disposes" (TLB). You see, God has a unique plan for each and every one of us and He is the only One sovereign, the only one truly in control.

Ever since I first read that verse I have strived to get to the point of serenity just a little beyond what we pray for each week. I'd like to acknowledge that my Higher Power is not only in control of what I cannot change but that He is also in control of what I can change.

I believe we have free will and God allows us to make our plans and live them out even when they aren't the best, even when we totally screw up. But every once in a while He exercises His sovereign authority and changes the plan. I must believe He loves me and that no matter what comes my way, good or bad, it is all good.

That is an easy thing to profess when everything is going according to plan or when what He changes causes things to turn out even better than I ever hoped for. It's not so easy when it brings my plans crashing about my ears and I have to give up something I may have been striving for many years and is very close to my heart. Or when I find I may not have as many years to live my plans as I thought because I end up with a terminal disease and my years are cut short. Or someone I dearly love passes away. No, it's not easy; but if I cannot trust God when the world falls apart around me, then I'm not really trusting Him at all.

God is the great provider, but His ways are beyond me and He often does things contrary to the wisdom of the age (and by that I mean mine). Who would have thought that His greatest provision for us would come in the form of a tiny baby, born in a barnyard, who would grow up to profess that the only way to true fulfillment and happiness was not in putting our own selves forward but in serving others. And, because of the simple truths He was preaching, the authority of that day would want to kill him. And they did kill Him, in a most cruel way. But it was all good, and because of that death, today we have a hope and a future.

But God doesn't just provide for the big things in our lives, He also provides the small. Like this token we are about to partake in that He gave to His disciples on the very night He was to suffer for us. He broke the bread and told them, "This is my body given for you" (Luke 22:19b) and, "this cup is the new covenant in my blood which is poured out for you" (Luke 22:20). Before He suffered and died, He prepared His disciples for what would happen when their plans came crashing down about them.

And He did one more thing. He told them, "...do this in remembrance of Me" (Luke 22:19c). He told them to remember Him, not because He would be dead and gone. No. He told them to remember Him because He was about to die and yet He would overcome even death—would still be with them as He is with us tonight, right here by my side. And there is nothing that can prevail against Him.

If I can reach that place of serenity then I don't have to look behind me to see the footsteps in the sand or see what the future holds in store. No, I can rest in the now, no matter my circumstances, without fear because I know He loves me, and all things happen for my good.

Tonight, as you come to share in this meal, take a moment to remember. And as you remember, no matter what circumstance you find yourself in, be encouraged.

Remember
Emily Joy Kelley, June 7, 2008
(the day of her baptism at 8 years old)

Hi, I'm Emily, and I'm a kid. I'm going to tell you what communion is about. I think Jesus gave it for a reminder to remember everything about Him. He wants us to remember that He died on the cross just because He loves us.

When I take communion I get a special feeling inside because I remember everything Jesus did for me, and I want you to have that feeling too when you take communion today. When you take communion today, remember Jesus loves you [point], and you [point], and you, and all of us. [point] Even you, Papa John.

My Friend Charlie
Bruce Andrews, March 6, 2009

Hi! My name is Bruce, and I'd like to invite the children to come up here and gather around me on the steps.

Kids, how old do you think I am? Guess. — I'm 81 years old, which is about twice as old as your mother; but once I was your age.

How many of you can swim? —Well, when I was your age, I could not swim, but I loved to play in the water.

Okay, how many of you have a best friend? —When I was your age I had a best friend. His name was Charlie Baity. When I was your age my family went on vacation to the Gulf of Mexico. My parents said I could invite my best friend Charlie Baity to go with us.

The first morning, my best friend Charlie and I went down to the beach to play in the water. When we got there, my sister was already in the water with a whole bunch of other kids. They were way out from the beach, but the water was only up to their chest. My best friend, Charlie and I walked out on a pier along side them until we were out as far as they were. I figured the water would not be over my head so I jumped in without taking a breath or anything. When I hit the water I kept going down, and down, until I finally hit the bottom. The water surface was way over my head. I had jumped into a hole they had dug so the boats would not be grounded when they were at the pier. Well, I just turned toward the pier and started walking on the bottom. But pretty soon I needed air, so I pushed off the bottom and, when my head came up, I took a breath of air but immediately sank back to the bottom where I started walking up the side of that hole. And as I'd run out of air, I'd push off again, come up and take another breath, then sink back down. Each time, as I came up, I'd thrust my hand straight up over my head, and finally when I got close enough to the pier my best friend, Charlie, grabbed my hand and helped me out of the water.

Years later, when I was as old as your mother, I developed a bad sickness. They call it hypoglycemia. When you have hypoglycemia, your blood sugar can get very low and you become very weak and can even faint. While I had hypoglycemia, I met Jesus and He became my Savior. He also became my Best Friend. And you know what? Whenever my hypoglycemia would bother me, do you know what I'd do? Well, in my mind I'd just reach my hand up and my Best Friend, Jesus, would take ahold of it and help me, and everything would be all right. After a year or so my Best Friend Jesus healed me of my hypoglycemia; but I had learned that whenever I was in any kind of trouble, He was always there. So, in my mind, I'd reach my hand up and He would take it and help me.

My challenge to you children is to make Jesus your Best Friend, and whenever you are in any kind of trouble, realize that your Best Friend Jesus is always there. In your mind, just reach your hand up and He will help you.

Now, I want to say something to the rest of the people here. If you haven't made Jesus your Best Friend, you can do that tonight. He is waiting for you right up there at His table which we are about to go to for communion. While you are there, you can make a commitment to make Him your Best Friend.

I'm Bruce. Thanks for letting me share about my best friend Charlie Baity and my Best Friend Jesus.

Beyond Berlin
Jason Kelley, 2009

I was recently in Berlin. As I was visiting the area where the wall once stood to separate people from each other, I realized there are many kinds of walls that separate people from each other and us from God. He wants all the walls to come down, not just the concrete ones.

Listen to the words [of this song] as we sing it through once, then the table will be open for you to take communion. Let Him speak to you as you come.

Beyond Berlin
by Jason Kelley

VERSE:
The world made a wall between us all, but You told it to fall
Now our hearts are burning,
We're desperately yearning to be where You are
We need freedom from the chains that keep us
From hearing Your voice when You call
We're tired of standing in place
Lord, we've tasted Your grace
Now we want it all

CHORUS:
You made the wall fall down, now make the chains fall off.
Free our hearts, Lord. Fill our souls, Lord.
You made the wall fall down, now make the chains fall off.
Free our hearts, Lord. Fill our souls, Lord.

VERSE:
The world made a wall between us all, but You told it to fall
Now our hearts are burning,
We're desperately yearning to be where You are
We need freedom from the chains that keep us
From hearing Your voice when You call
We're tired of standing in place
Lord, we've tasted Your grace
Now we want it all

CHORUS:
You made the wall fall down; now make the chains fall off.
Free our hearts, Lord. Fill our souls, Lord.
You made the wall fall down, now make the chains fall off.
Free our hearts, Lord. Fill our souls, Lord.

VERSE SEGMENT:
We need freedom from the chains that keep us
From hearing Your voice when You call
We're tired of standing in place
Lord, we've tasted Your grace
Now we want it all.

ENDING:

Free our hearts, Lord
Fill our souls, Lord
Free our hearts, Lord
Fill our souls, Lord

FREEDOM ISN'T FREE
Aunt Laurie, January 2010

When I look at this table I'm reminded that Freedom isn't free. I hear that phrase all the time. It costs us something to live free in a perilous world. Having loved ones in the military I have the constant clenching of my heart to remind me of the price of that freedom. This table reminds me of a more crucial Freedom.

> "Jesus said, 'If you hold to My teaching, you are really My disciples. Then you will know the truth, and the truth will set you free'" (John 8:31-32).

The people Jesus was talking to were insulted. They didn't believe they were in bondage—they believed their genealogy made them free. We might think we are not in bondage because we live in America, or we're wealthy, or some other reason; but Jesus went on to say that they (we) are enslaved by sin, we are all equal in that respect.

However Jesus did not leave it there. He went on to say, "So if the Son sets you free, you will be free indeed" (John 8:36). Jesus set us free from the bondage of sin which carries with it the bondage of performing enough good deeds to pay for our sin. The Good News is that our *Freedom* is bought and paid for.

The Apostle Paul put it this way in Galatians 5:1:

> "Christ has set us free. Stand firm, then, and do not let yourselves be burdened again by a yoke of slavery."

Paul was talking to people who were adding requirements to the Good News: "Rely on Christ *and* do this" to be free. But there is no "this." All we need is on the table.

Paul went on to say:

> "You, my brothers and sisters, were called to be free. But do not use your freedom to indulge the flesh; rather, serve one another humbly in love. For the entire law is fulfilled in keeping this one command: 'Love your neighbor as yourself'" (Gal. 5:13-14).

This table reminds me of what it cost to gain my spiritual freedom—the freedom to walk in loving, graceful fellowship with Creator God (and those He brings across my path)—because He paid the price in full for me with His body, and His blood.

The Eyes of the Lord
Pat Widhalm, May 22, 2010

Hi, I'm Pat. I'm an Overcomer.

I love being a part of Serenity Church—miracles happen here. I can't wait to spend time with you. "You Rock!"

About a week-and-a-half ago I was scheduled to have surgery to remove a cancer growing inside of me, and I was planning to use the resultant hole in me as an object lesson to lead into what I want to talk about. However, due to circumstances beyond my surgeon's or my control, my surgery has been postponed. So tonight I still have the cancer but I don't have my hole!

But being a resourceful design engineer, I just happen to have a backup plan. This is not my first encounter with cancer. About 20 years ago I had a rare form of cancer growing in one of the quadriceps muscles of my right leg. To remove the tumor they cut out the entire muscle. It left a scar and my leg deformed, which is one reason I don't wear shorts and flip-flops like John does. Well, actually it is a reason I don't wear shorts; I don't wear flip-flops because I can't stand that thongy thing between my toes.

After all these years, the wound still causes me pain and, due to the missing muscle, sometimes my leg buckles and I stumble, even fall on my face. Not many people are aware of the pain and embarrassment that wound causes me, but I am!

I look out over all the people here tonight and I see you, but I don't see you like God sees you. I can't see your heart, but I believe the majority of you could say what I just did. Your wound may not be a visible wound, but the invisible wound is often deeper, more painful, and much more difficult to heal. Whether this is your first time here or you consider yourself a regular, if that is the condition you find yourself in, welcome home. You have come to the right place. Miracles happen here.

Unless this is your first time with us, chances are good you have heard John tell us, at one time or another, about one of his "favorite" hymns he sang ages ago when, he claims, he was actually young. It is about the "All-Seeing Eye" and he sings a little of it like this: "There is an all-seeing eye, watching youuu, watching youuu...." That is one creepy song, and if John sings it for you it is even more eerie. He will tell you that song always freaked him out because he was always doing things he should not do and did not want anyone knowing about, especially that all-seeing eye. He thought he was somehow unique in his ability to do those "bad" things.

Is anyone else here capable of such things? Some of us are probably in denial and some of us are too proud to admit it. It was a trick question with no right answer.

It is easy to think God is like that—setting up an impossible standard then waiting for us to screw up so He can grind us into the ground like an old cigarette butt. That is what we expect from the world around us. After all, in Matthew 5:48 even Jesus said, "Be perfect, therefore, as your heavenly Father is perfect." That is a tough standard.

There may be some people who haven't heard the Good News, and the rest of us tend to forget that Christ performed the greatest miracle of all time for us. It is so transforming we celebrate it every time we share this communion meal. He died for *all* of the sins of the world—past, eminently pending, and all that will be done in the future by all of the people ever born or who ever will be born in this entire troubled world. He offers that to us as a free gift, and when we accept what He did for us, He takes away the burden of our sin and lays on us the mantle of His holy perfection so, when He sees us, all He sees is a pure heart committed to Him.

But there is some truth in that creepy hymn of John's. Linda pointed out to me a scripture in 2 Chronicles that had a profound impact on me.

> For the eyes of the Lord range throughout the earth to strengthen those whose hearts are fully committed to Him (2 Chron.16:9a).

God is not looking to zap us because we have weak moments, even if we don't trust Him. Mercy, no! He knows us better than we know ourselves, and He loves us still and draws us to His Son (Jeremiah 31:3)—and you can take that one to the bank.

But He is looking for opportunities to strengthen us in the very midst of our weakness, and that is a miracle, too! Granted, sometimes it is like a surgeon's knife cutting deep to remove a cancer that would eventually kill us, and it hurts like crazy! But sometimes, it is the soft touch and sweet embrace of a friend when we are afraid, the touch that lets us know we aren't alone, that gives us strength to face our fear. But He always works in our lives with loving kindness.

And God is not limited in the way He works that miracle. In my experience He most often gives that strength through the people He brings into our lives. And this community of brothers and sisters, this family we call Serenity, is a perfect display of that miracle.

Hebrews 10:25 tells us not to give up meeting together but to encourage one another all the more, whether that be during our celebration service or in Overcomers, or when just two or three are gathered together in His name. First Corinthians tells us how we do that:

> "When you come together, each one has a song, has a lesson, has a revelation, has a tongue, has an interpretation. Let all these things be done for the strengthening of the church" (1 Corinthians 14:26 NET).

And we are the church! So when we sing, participate in devotions such as this, listen to the message, and, most especially, when we pray for one another, we are strengthening each other in our weaknesses, and then we can do all things through our Higher Power, Jesus Christ, who strengthens us.

What better way to focus on that truth than through this meal we are about to share. Food strengthens us. Now, don't expect that little piece of bread and that splash of juice to literally fill you up. Those elements are just the corporal symbol of the real spiritual meal it represents; it serves to remind us of Christ's sacrifice that made this feast possible. That is why this is the most scared time in this fellowship celebration tonight. To me, it is like the blessing over the meal where we give thanks for the One who provides for us; but it is only part of this incredible spiritual feast we have already been partaking.

Along with exercising by what you take in, the best way to keep your strength up is to keep eating. Therefore, "Keep coming back. It works if you work it and it won't if you don't!"

"IT'S OKAY, MAMA. THEY NEED IT!"
Aunt Laurie, February 2011

My belief is that I'm not worthy to come to this table because of some list of good I have accomplished. I'm worthy by virtue of an *invitation*.

Tonight I want to share with you some experiences I had as a child regarding communion. We usually went to church with my grandmother, who never missed a service. When the tray of broken saltines and cups of juice were passed at grandma's little church, the children were allowed to participate. I loved the miniature glass cups of grape juice and unexpected snack during church. That was what communion meant to me: an unexpected snack.

One time we attended a different church with some cousins. They passed a tray of perfectly formed little oyster crackers, and I reached to take one like I did at Grandma's church. My hand was slapped hard and I was told, "No! You don't do that!" I watched the tray of tiny juice cups passing by, feeling ashamed and confused. It is strange how that memory makes me want to sit up straight and rub the back of my hand!

Another experience was with my babysitter, Mrs. Toffoli, when I was about nine years old. She, along with her husband and three children, attended church sometimes with me and my brother and sister in tow. The first time we went with them there was an obvious dilemma: what to do with us heathens when the family went forward to receive communion. They could not leave us there by ourselves because, really, we were not trustworthy! I still remember what Papa Toffoli said: "It's okay, Mama. They need it!" So it was settled. Mrs. Toffoli, Papa Toffoli, and six children went forward to receive communion.

Maybe some of us here have been slapped away in one way or another from this table, but the truth is we are welcome here because Jesus threw the door open and made the invitation—not because we deserve it, but because, just like Papa Toffoli said, we need it. This is what Communion means to me.

No Barriers
Pat Widhalm, June 2011

I'm Pat, and I'm an Overcomer. The last time I spoke was last year at our Sereniversary, and Uncle Bill thought it would be a good tradition if I spoke again this year. We have some strange traditions here, but we are a very loving family and traditions are important to family—even the strange ones.

If you haven't yet experienced what family means here, you will, because the moment you walked through that door you were considered part of the family. Welcome home!

When I was preparing what I would say last year, I was anticipating that I would have just recently completed an operation to cure me of prostate cancer and I was planning to use that as a talking point. The problem was, though, the surgery was delayed and I had to change my approach. Good thing, too! I had very naive expectations about that surgery and it was several weeks before I could even stand up. No way I would have been able to become a tradition last year if my surgery had gone as scheduled.

About the same time, I lost my father by marriage and dear friend by love, Bruce Andrews, to the same disease my surgery cured me of. As Bruce was dying I would sit by his side. I watched the pain he endured and, by comparison, my suffering seemed like a simple paper cut. Those experiences and others from this past year have left me more subdued than I was, and I have been giving more thought to just how much my Savior loves me—and how much He loves you!

Before Jesus was crucified, He was scourged with a cat-o'-nine-tails—traditionally "39 lashes less one" so scourging, itself, would not kill the one being punished. A scourging was designed to painfully tear the flesh to shreds (surgery is designed to make the smallest scar possible with as little pain as possible).

He then had a crown of the thorns pressed deeply down on his head and, in spite of the great pain He was already enduring, He was forced to carry the very instrument of his death through a throng of people. The intent was to bring shame. The cross was the most cruel torture ever devised. It induced a slow and agonizing death, more pain than even Bruce endured.

And Jesus was not naive, like I had been. At the Last Supper He knew what He would endure for us. Later, in great anguish, when He prayed in the garden, sweating drops of blood, He pled three times "Father, if it is possible, may this cup be taken from me" (Matthew 26:39b), but each time He willingly accepted the cup for our sake.

The Last Supper was the Jewish Passover meal, or Seder service, and by tradition there are four cups presented, each representing a different aspect of God's salvation plan: the Sanctification Cup, Deliverance Cup, Redemption cup, and Praise cup. Tradition says it was the Redemption cup that Jesus shared with His disciples, the cup of His blood that would be shed for us that would create a new covenant of grace and mercy. After sharing the Redemption cup, Jesus refused the fourth cup saying He would not drink again of the fruit of the vine until the covenant was fulfilled and He could drink it again with us in the Kingdom of Heaven.

With His last words on the cross—"It is finished!" (John 19:30)—the Kingdom of Heaven overcame our sin and and was established here on earth. It is that fourth cup, the cup of Praise, that is on the table here tonight as we remember what He has done for us.

This is a very sacred moment in our service tonight and in some churches their tradition doesn't allow you to share in this meal unless you are "holy" enough. But "What do I know of holy?"

There is a song by Addison Road with that title ["What Do I Know of Holy." *Addison Road*. 2008] that speaks very much to my heart. I'm not going to make you suffer by singing it for you but it will be playing as you take communion. I did not write the words but they are mine as well; perhaps they are yours, too. There is something of Him you can know. Knowledge grows with each encounter. Jesus loves you beyond your wildest imaginations. He suffered and died to open His arms to us. There are absolutely no barriers between us and His love except the ones we build ourselves. You don't have to be holy to merit His love, or to share in this meal or the gifts He has for you. You only have to want to be loved.

Whether your understanding of who Jesus is and what this meal is about is like Aunt Laurie's when she was a little girl—a nice little unexpected snack, or like Eve's where you feel the presence of God because you asked to, know that you are welcome at His table. Wherever you find yourself, on a mountain top or in a deep, ugly pit, know that if you take a step toward Jesus He will rush to you with open arms, wherever you are. So come, share this meal with us.

I'm Pat. Thanks for listening to me.

COMPARISONS TO OUR PARENTHOOD
Lisa Watson, July 2, 2011

When Gideon was a couple of weeks old I handed him to Joel and told him, "I'm going to take a shower. The baby will be hungry soon but I should have enough time to take a shower first." Of course, I was in the shower about three-and-a-half seconds and the baby started crying. I hurried as fast as I could but by the time I was out Gideon was crying that heartbreaking, frantic, newborn cry.

I remember finally being able to sit down and nurse him. I can't describe how incredibly happy and privileged I felt to get to be the one who made it all better. At that moment I heard God say to me, "This is exactly how I feel when you come to Me with your problems."

He showed me some comparisons to our parenthood:

I had to sacrifice my own body to bear a child. A lot of not-so-pretty things happen to your body during pregnancy.

Labor and delivery are incredibly painful. And while the whole ordeal was ugly at times, it was also one of the most beautiful things in the world! Jesus gave the ultimate bodily sacrifice. His beating and crucifixion was the ugliest. But it was also the most beautiful.

I brought one life into an ugly world. He made it possible for every life to enter the most beautiful world.

I can't nurse a baby without first going through the pregnancy and the labor. He could not offer us this meal without first going through the crucifixion.

We both waited in expectation for the day we would endure horrible pain because we knew the end result would be worth it.

Once my labor started there was no turning back. I could not change my mind. Gideon was born at home so there were not even any drug options. I had to endure it to the finish. Once the beatings and the mocking and the hammering of nails started, Jesus still had a choice. He could change His mind. But He did not.

While I was enduring labor I was surrounded by my husband, my mom, my sisters, and my midwives. None of them could take the pain away, but they were there to be with me and do what they could to support me. When Jesus hung on the cross His friends deserted Him and His Father turned His back on Him. He went through it alone.

I went through labor so that Gideon and I could live separate from each other. Jesus died so we could be together.

Gideon has made quite a few messes since he was born three months ago. He has had poop up to his ears and down to his toes. And I was happy to clean it up. I knew if he just sat in it, it would irritate him, give him a rash, and make him miserable. We have all been in a mess that irritated us, gave us a rash, and made us miserable. And all we have to do is cry out and Jesus will come running with his bag of wipes and clean clothes.

I look at Gideon and I see an adorable baby I'm sure anyone would love to take care of. I don't see myself the same way. But once we are wrapped in Jesus' blood, all He sees is the precious face of His sweet little baby. And He can't wait to snuggle us up and offer His body as nourishment for our lives.

OUR BIGGER PICTURE
Aunt Laurie, September 2011

I'm Aunt Laurie, and I'm an Overcomer.

> "I have told you these things, so that in Me you may have peace. In this world you will have trouble. But take heart! I have overcome the world" (John 16:33).

My day job is high stress most of the time. Sometimes I get so wound up in that stress I have to stop myself, take a deep breath, make myself remember what is really important. I usually look at the pictures on the window sill behind my desk—all my kids, grandkids, and this man [hold up picture of husband, Bill]. I can be absolutely freaked out about deadlines and work loads, but one look at this face and I'm okay.

[indicate table] This table is our Bigger Picture. This table is our picture of Jesus. This picture brings me back from the edge of "busy" and "worry" and brings me into remembrance of Jesus. This picture reminds me that He gave all to restore me to sanity. He gave all.

Life is full of pressure, stress, and distractions. Jesus knew we needed a time of remembrance. This table is my time to stop and remember what is really important. This table is the picture that gives me true hope.

Rats in the Cellar
Pat Widhalm, December 2011

Hi, I'm Pat. I'm an Overcomer. We are a strange lot, we humans. Absolutely unique, no one exactly the same and yet we are much the same.

We have a certain temperament ingrained within us at birth by the genes we inherited from our parents. They say there are four basic temperament types but for me it really boils down to two. Extroverts, like John, are very outgoing and people oriented. Introverts, like me, are less people oriented and more inwardly directed. What our specific temperament might be is really some blend from one of those extremes to the other.

We have certain abilities and talents; some of those are a part of our genetics and some are learned and developed. Our temperament and talents are rather like filters for how we see and interact with the world around us.

We are all God's creation. At our conception we were instilled with our temperaments and our talents to fulfill a very high purpose: reflect the glory of God.

We humans are capable of unselfish love and great good, as is our purpose. We laud those higher qualities in our fellow man and we like to shine a light on our goodness because God is light and we are part of the light. But we are also rather a paradox because there is a dark part of us deep within our core that we don't like to acknowledge and, in fact, often deny entirely. We put on fronts of righteousness much like the Pharisees of old.

C. S. Lewis referred to that darkness within as "the rats in the cellar" because rats scurry around in the darkness doing ugly things but quickly hide from the light. That deep, dark place within us is more vast than outer space, extends to eternity, and is mostly unexplored. It is like the area on mariners' charts of old that depicted unexplored places with the notation, "Here be dragons!"

I think I really became aware of that inner darkness when I was in high school, "coming of age." I refer to it as my "dark beast" because what it is capable of scares me and I have tried to keep it hidden and locked away. My dark beast is all of my passions and emotions that make me capable of doing great harm to those around me, especially to those I love.

Try as I might, I have found that I can't keep the beast chained. As Paul says in Romans, I do what I don't want to do. If you know what I'm talking about, say "Amen." Yes, you do, because most of you have accepted that we are broken people, and you have faced the beast within you and no longer delude yourselves that it is not there.

So, is the beast Satan-contrived and, like Flip Wilson, we can say "The devil made me do it?" Heavens, no! Satan does not have the power to create anything. Only God can create, and I will not give Satan what is God's due.

I'm God's creation only and, similar to Popeye, I declare, "I am what I am and that's all that I am!" All of those passions and emotions are a God-given part of me and essential to my purpose in this world. But, as C. S. Lewis noted in *Out Of the Silent Planet*, we are a bent people and there is hidden within us a darkness at our very core that perverts what God intended for good.

We are called to be servants to one another but we have bent that calling from "seeking to serve" to "seeking to be served." That bentness has brought a great deal of sorrow and suffering into our world. Like Paul, we each can say "I am the chief among sinners. What a wretch I am!" (1 Timothy 1:15).

But there is hope because we have a God who truly loves us in spite of our wretchedness. We talk about the 12 Promises and they are good, but the promises of God are unlimited. Perhaps we have to limit our view because, like that deep, dark place within us, we can't comprehend the vastness of God's love for us. All we have to do to claim His promises is to ask. It is simple but it is not easy, and we can't do it alone.

That is why God sent us His Son, Jesus, our Higher Power, to do the work of amends for us. His Spirit dwells within the very heart of that deep, dark cellar where the rats and the dragons reside. It is His Spirit who tames the dragons. And He gave us His Word from which we learn the way out of darkness through the 12 Steps—with each of us holding up the other as we walk side by side, encouraging one another through our failings, and learning what it means to serve one another.

That is love, and that is what we celebrate through this communion.We are reminded that Christ died for us to give us the power to overcome the darkness within us, to love one another, and to forgive as He does— to serve Him by serving others. What joy there is in service to our God!

I'm Pat. Thanks for listening to me.

STIRRING UP HUNGER
Aunt Laurie, January 2012

Around Serenity Church I'm known as Aunt Laurie, and I'm an Overcomer.

I don't know about you, but for me, the last few weeks have been a season of Eating. We don't just eat, we celebrate eating! Has anyone besides me, sometime in the last few weeks, felt so full you were sure you would never eat again? But a little bit later we start remembering how good it was and, next thing you know, we are rummaging in the refrigerator looking for leftovers because we are hungry again!

We come to the table when we are hungry. Sometimes we are ravenously hungry and can't wait for the table to be set. But sometimes we don't realize how hungry we are until we see the table spread. And just like the sight of a Thanksgiving or Christmas feast stirs our hunger, the sight of this table stirs our spiritual hunger when we stop and remember what this meal represents.

Jesus said:

> "You're blessed when you've lost it all. God's kingdom is there for the finding.
>
> You're blessed when you're ravenously hungry. Then you're ready for the Messianic meal.
>
> You're blessed when the tears flow freely. Joy comes with the morning" (Luke 6:20-21 *The Message*).

This meal represents God doing for me what I could not do for myself. This meal represents satisfaction I could find nowhere else. This meal turns my sorrow into joy.

Come to this table because you are hungry. Come to this table to celebrate. Come to this table because you remember how good He is. He invites you to this table.

USING THE SONG "TO BELIEVE"
Linda Widhalm, April 7, 2012

Hello, Serenity Church! My name is Linda, and I'm an Overcomer! Welcome, each of you. I'm very glad you are here tonight so we can celebrate together the most victorious day of all time: Easter. The day Jesus rose up from the dead. His body that was broken for us but rose up and came out from the tomb.

Before we share together the meal we eat in remembrance of Jesus, I'm very happy to be able to share with you a very special song, sung by a very special little girl, Jackie Evancho, and written by her uncle, Matthew Evancho. The song is a prayer. Let's listen prayerfully. [Play "To Believe" from the album *Dream with Me*, Peer International. 2011.]

While you were listening did some person, some experience, some situation, some group of people come to mind? Someone you would help if you could? Someone you might have helped in some way but did not? Is there someone you have had a heart connection with in the past that you wonder about now? Someone struggling with their faith, their sobriety, their life? Someone who tugs at your heart?

Hold on to the answer to that question while I explain how we will be sharing communion together tonight. When you come forward to take communion, you will be given two pieces of bread. Let the first one represent your remembrance of Jesus, celebrating the victory He has given you. Then let the second be for the one or ones who tug at your heart, those people whom you want Jesus to remember and bless, especially today. Those not as fortunate as you in spirit, faith, or physical comfort. Dip it in the cup on their behalf, be free to speak aloud their name or situation as you remember them to Jesus, then eat.

[Hold up the Bread] This is His body given as a sacrifice for us. This is His body for a broken world.

[Hold up the Cup] This is His blood shed for you. This is His blood shed for the world.

Please come quietly as the song replays then return quietly to your seat until all have shared the meal. The table is open! [Replay "To Believe"]

PERSPECTIVE
Pat Widhalm, May 2012

Hi. My name is Pat, and I'm an Overcomer.

When my kids were very young, one of my favorite things to do was read stories to them. I liked to try and get into the story and become each of the characters to make the story come alive for them. I would try to see the story through the eyes of the characters, so I'd speak and tell the story the way I thought the characters would. Apparently I was pretty good at it because all my kids have shared with me what an impact that made on their lives. I kind of like that, so I have continued the tradition with my grandkids.

I remember one time when my oldest granddaughter, Emily, was just a little girl, she was sitting on my lap and I was reading a story to her. After a bit, it became obvious to me that she really was not listening but seemed fascinated with my hair; she was running her fingers through the hair on the back of my head (one of the few places I still have some). So I stopped reading and I asked her if something was wrong. She told me, "Oh no, Papa, I was just looking at all of your beautiful white hair. But, why did you cut the hole in the top?"

I smiled, but really I was overcome with love and well pleased with Emily at that moment because she turned the table on me and for just a moment I got a chance to see myself from her perspective. I was beautiful and totally in control of everything, even the hole in my head. What a rare and special gift. She believes in me, and I want to do anything I can for her so she always will!

Jesus said, "Truly I tell you, unless you change and become like little children, you will never enter the kingdom of heaven" (Matthew 18:3). I think Jesus was referring to perspective. For several reasons, and for some time now, God has been dealing with me on the subject of perspective, and I'd like to share with you some of what I have discovered.

We live in a "Me first" society and are taught that the only correct perspective is Mine—everything is about me and revolves around what I need, but it is okay if all of the rest of you come second. So, no matter what someone else's intentions might be toward me, unless they fit my perceived need they become an attack on all that is right and good in the world.

I think that is why God is not so popular with those who hold that worldview. He is a killjoy rather than someone who wants the best for me and those around me. And I believe it is the same "Me First" perspective that tarnishes our relationships with one another.

As a Christian, I thought I had overcome that attitude; but I recently discovered I'm not as immune as I thought. In Philippians 2:3 Paul tells us, "Do nothing out of selfish ambition or vain conceit. Rather, in humility, value others above yourselves." Paul was talking to a family of believers such as we are here at Serenity. In a family, Love (with a capital "L") is the glue. In the world's view, it is "every man for himself" and you are right to be cynical about what the world says to you. But here, we have something special.

God said He is Love, and He puts His Spirit of Love within those of us who acknowledge Jesus is Lord. Love is not easy. Sometimes it has hard things to say to us and requires hard choices from us—though they are never intended to hurt us, only to lift us up. If we hold to a self-centered perspective, however, it is easy to distort what we interpret from those around us who love us. I know, because I'm very self-centered and I get things wrong all the time.

I have recently discovered a little higher perspective. It is only a little higher, but it is making a positive difference in my relationships with those I love. I have discovered that I'm very prone to react with a worldview perspective to what is said to me. I have learned that if I allow Him, God has given me the ability to pause and take a step back and see through the eyes of the ones who love me. I don't always completely agree with what is said, but I have found that if I take the perspective Paul talks about and consider the one speaking to me as better than myself, I can always find truth in what is said; and that truth is worthy of my consideration. I believe this new perspective is making me a better person.

Having said all that, I'd like to ask you to look at this communion meal tonight from a different perspective. Look at it as a story being read to you by someone who loves you perfectly. This is our story, but it is one that Jesus put Himself into to make it come alive as it was meant to be.

There is so much evil and suffering in the world. We blame it on God, asking, "How can a loving, all-powerful God allow this?" But as we cry out for justice, if we honestly answer the question "What is wrong with the world?" we must face the fact that the best answer we can give is "I am"—I am what is wrong with the world.

Jesus is what is right with the world. If you truly understand what He did by becoming part of our story, you may want to cry, as some stories of injustice can make you do, because a perfect Jesus had to die in our place for the evil all of us have done. And He did it so that we might live. His death opened us up for His spirit to live within us so we don't have to settle for what the world offers.

Each day is a new day, and each day His spirit gives us the power to see life from a higher perspective. Through that, we can overcome all our failings. Maybe you didn't make it today and maybe we won't tomorrow, or the next; but know this: whether you believe in God or not, God believes in you, and from His perspective you are beautiful. He has the will and the power to bring you to perfection.

What a great story we have because of Jesus! And it is a true story. God loves you that much! So come, and as you share this meal with us I want to leave you with this question to consider:

Knowing God believes in you and has made Himself a part of your story, what will you do with that? How will you honor Him?

In the Presence of Mine Enemies
Linda Widhalm, June 2012

Hi! My name is Linda, and I'm an Overcomer.

Psalm 23. A psalm of David.

The Lord is my shepherd, I lack nothing.
  He makes me lie down in green pastures,
  He leads me beside quiet waters,
  He refreshes my soul.

He guides me along the right paths for His name's sake.

Even though I walk through the darkest valley,
  I will fear no evil,
  for You are with me;
  Your rod and Your staff, they comfort me.

You prepare a table before me in the presence of my enemies. You
  anoint my head with oil;
  my cup overflows.

Surely Your goodness and love will follow me
  All the days of my life,
  And I will dwell in the house of the Lord forever.

A few months ago, actually while I was preparing the last Communion Meditation I gave at Easter, I was struggling with a deep wound in my life which was hindering me from getting it together. I cried out to the Lord to give me peace. Then I realized the words of the 23rd Psalm were running through my head, so I began praying them in my heart.

That is when the Lord gave the 23rd Psalm new meaning for me. He gently said to me, "My table, this table, is the one I prepare before you in the presence of your enemies. I serve it to both of you."

Please bow your head for a moment of silent meditation while the servers are being served.

REMEMBER, RELEASE, RECEIVE
Alisa Spears, July 2012

Hi. I'm Alisa, and I'm an Overcomer. I want to be purposeful about explaining this and bringing us back to our roots, its history, the meaning, but also in how it relates to us right now and everyday. As we come to the table, I want to take a moment and remind us what this means to us as individuals and as a community.

This meal for us is a place to remember, release, and receive.

We remember: That Jesus died on the cross for us so we could be forgiven, and our relationship with God could be made right. We remember that our sin is what placed Jesus on the cross. It was me and you who broke the heart of God, over and over again. But Jesus acted on our behalf. I want to come back to this part about Jesus acting on our behalf in a minute and explain how He still acts on our behalf.

We release our burdens and remember that Jesus says He will *never* leave us. We lay down our pride, our frustration, our sin—and we do this by pausing before we come, to say, "Lord, here I am. I lay my life at your feet. And in the places that I can't, give me the courage and strength to do so."

And we receive the loving embrace of the Father, the Son, and the Spirit. We receive a new identity. We are no longer people defined by our stuff, our mess, but we are God's beloved child. *You* are God's beloved child.

After you come and get your bread and dip it in the juice, eat this meal slowly, receive the grace and love of your heavenly Father. Before we do this, though, I want to go back to the part about how Jesus acted on our behalf. How He still acts on our behalf.

Daily, I fall short. Daily, I have flaws that shine through. Yet I'm forgiven and loved, not only by God but by His body of believers. He calls *us* to be this body, to be His body. To love ourselves and others.

When I'm deep in my hurt, I try to remember by closing my eyes and picturing how much Jesus must have been hurt when He walked through the crowd carrying the cross He would hang on. I think about how much more His heart must have hurt than mine does. I think about those that He loved mocking Him, cursing Him, turning their backs on Him during the most desperate moments. Despite all of that, He loved every one of them. He loved us and still sacrificed Himself. He gave no excuse, only love.

Then I prepare to release. With my eyes closed I picture God's arms wrapped around me as I lay down my burdens, my hurt, stresses, and mess. I listen for God's voice. With my eyes closed and still picturing God's arms wrapped around me, I receive His word and listen as He says, "I will not leave you. I forgive you, and I love you." I receive forgiveness as my heart feels full of God's love. Once my heart is full and I have let go and received, I open my eyes and feel renewed.

Prayer attributed to St. Francis of Assisi:

*L*ord, make me a channel of Thy peace
  that where there is hatred, I may bring love;
    that where there is wrong, I may bring
      the spirit of forgiveness;
    that where there is discord, I may bring harmony;
    that where there is error, I may bring truth;
    that where there is doubt, I may bring faith;
    that where there is despair, I may bring hope;
    that where there are shadows, I may bring light;
    that where there is sadness, I may bring joy.

Lord, grant that I may seek rather
  to comfort than to be comforted;
  to understand, than to be understood;
  to love, than to be loved.

For it is by self-forgetting that one finds.
  It is by forgiving that one is forgiven.
  It is by dying that one awakens to eternal life.

Amen.

Brothers, If Someone Is Caught in a Sin
Aunt Laurie, September 2012

> Brothers and sisters, if someone is caught in a sin, you who live by
> the Spirit should restore that person gently. But watch yourselves,
> or you also may be tempted (Galatians 6:1).

Sound familiar? I have heard this scripture read hundreds of times over
the last six years. I did not give it much thought until I came up here
and read the 12 Steps a couple of weeks ago. I had always assumed it
meant when we spiritual people *catch* someone sinning, we bend our
haloed-heads down and lift our brother or sister up to our level. But a
couple of weeks ago when I said, "if someone is *caught*," I saw a spider
web.

Sin is like a spider web. Sin is what catches people, not me. The message
of this verse is humility; not the pride that would stoop to lift a brother
up, but the love and humility that would come near and offer a gentle
hand out of the web.

And why must I keep an attentive eye on myself? What is my
temptation? Anytime you reach out to restore someone, it is possible
the person is not ready to be restored. They could be so self-deceived
and tangled in delusion [act out being caught in web but in denial] that
they don't want to be free, or they deny that there is anything to be free
of.

When I'm reaching out to someone in denial, I must keep an attentive
eye on myself by walking in love and humility: *not judgment*. My
temptation is to judge, so that is what I watch for in myself, because
Paul also told the Galatians to endure each other's troublesome, moral
faults and that by doing so they would fulfill perfectly the law of Christ.

"Fulfill perfectly the law of Christ" sounds like a big deal to me. How
can I be a more spiritual Christian? It is clearly stated here: To fulfill
perfectly the law of Christ we endure the troublesome faults of others.

The next verses go on to instruct that we should not compare ourselves
to others or think we are better than them. If I'm not humbly patient
with your faults, I'm vulnerable to getting caught in the sin of judgment,
which *never restored anyone,* and is the opposite of the love and humility
that Jesus modeled for us here [indicate communion table].

Let's remember Him. He's the only solution for troublesome moral
faults.

Take What's Coming to You
The Palo Duro Canyon Story
Aunt Laurie, February 2, 2013

Then the King will say 'Enter, you who are blessed by My Father! Take what is coming to you in this kingdom. It has been ready for you since the world's foundation. And here's why:

I was hungry and you fed Me,
I was thirsty and you gave Me a drink,
I was a stranger and you welcomed Me,
I was shivering and you gave Me clothes,
I was sick and you stopped to visit,
I was in prison and you came to Me.

That is my adaptation of Matthew 25:34-36. My adaptation goes on in verses 37-40:

Then those 'sheep' are going to say, "Master, what are You talking about? When did we ever see You hungry and feed You, thirsty and give You a drink? And when did we ever see You sick or in prison and come to You?"

Then the King will say, "I'm telling the solemn truth: Whenever you did one of these things to someone overlooked or ignored, that was Me—you did it to Me."

Has anyone here ever been to Palo Duro Canyon in the panhandle of Texas? I went a few years ago with a friend. We set out to hike a six-mile trail on a hot summer day. There is a large warning sign at the trail head that gave advice on attire, gear, and water needed to complete the hike. I read the sign and my exact words were, "Pish posh!" I took one 16 ounce bottle, but my friend went back to the car for more water. She was cramming bottles into every pocket, her waistband, into her fanny pack. I went skipping down the trail with smug frivolity; after all, I was not weighted down with all of that extra water!

The day was hot, around 100 degrees. After an hour, I had lost all of the spring in my step. My water was gone and I was beginning to hallucinate. I collapsed in the meager shade of a juniper bush. At first I was stubborn about accepting water from my friend, but my friend convinced me she did not want to have to carry my dead carcass out of the canyon on her back, so for *her* sake, I accepted her help.

I did not prepare for that hike, even though the best advice for a successful hike was available. I got myself into that situation due to pride, thinking I was the exception to the rule. The natural course of events would have been for me to keel over from heat stroke. That is what I deserved. But my friend intervened in mercy. She gave me water, she fanned me with her hat, she shaded me with her body until I was able to get back on my feet. Because of her I made it out of the canyon that day.

Back to Matthew 25. The scripture doesn't say:

> I was hungry (due to no fault of my own) and you fed me,
> I was thirsty (even though I prepared for the worst) …
> I was a stranger (because unforeseen circumstances forced me from my home) and you welcomed me,
> I was shivering (because I was robbed by an evil person) …
> I was sick (even though I eat a perfectly nutritious diet, exercise regularly, get plenty of sleep and wash my hands 48 times a day)
> I was in prison (for something I didn't do) and you came to me.

There are no qualifiers in Jesus' list, and it is the same way at His table. Jesus doesn't say, "Come to My table if you are spiritually fit and have been fasting and praying all week." He says, "Come to My table because you have been watching TV and complaining all week. Come to my table broken, unprepared, feeling stupid, feeling weak, and hallucinating."

Coming to His table is not some kind of promenade of the righteous. We come to His table to remember that He is the answer to our broken, ill-prepared lives. We come to His table because He is the only hope we have.

Do You Want to Get Well?
Lisa Watson, March 9, 2013

John 5:1-9 says

> Sometime later, Jesus went up to Jerusalem for one of the Jewish festivals. Now there is in Jerusalem near the Sheep Gate a pool, which in Aramaic is called Bethesda and which is surrounded by five covered colonnades. Here a great number of disabled people used to lie—the blind, the lame, the paralyzed—and they waited for the moving of the waters.

> From time to time an angel of the Lord would come down and stir up the waters. The first person into the pool after each such disturbance would be cured of whatever disease they had.

> One who was there had been an invalid for thirty-eight years. When Jesus saw him lying there and learned that he had been in his condition for a long time, He asked him, "Do you want to get well?"

> "Sir," the invalid replied, "I have no one to help me into the pool when the water is stirred. While I'm trying to get in, someone else goes down ahead of me."

> Then Jesus said to him, "Get up! Pick up your mat and walk."

> At once the man was cured; he picked up his mat and walked.

We all have hurts or diseases that prevent us from living life as God intended. And Jesus asks each of us the same question He asked this man: "Do you want to get well?" We don't have to sit around a pool waiting on an angel and hoping to be the first one in, hoping to be the one who receives healing. Jesus' body and blood are always available. There is enough for everyone. You don't have to be first in line. The power never runs out. It is as great for the first in line as it will be for the very last.

Jesus is saying the same thing to each of us: "Get up! Clean up the things that have kept you comfortable in your illness, and come, accept your healing."

Resurrection and Redemption
Deborah (Helmstetler) Moravec, March 16, 2013

Hi, I'm Deborah. I'm an Overcomer.

Every time I take communion, or even think about communion, it takes me back to a time in my life when I was completely broken. I was down and out. I never thought there was a way to pick myself up by my bootstraps and keep on going. A time when I believed I could not continue on my own.

Even though I was not sure I deserved it, I *begged* God to take me back; *begged* for His forgiveness. I began to search. Through my little search I came across a scripture, 1 Timothy 1:15-16:

> Here is a trustworthy saying that deserves full acceptance: Christ Jesus came into the world to save sinners—of whom I am the very worst. But for that very reason I was shown mercy so that in me, the worst of all sinners, Christ Jesus might display His immense patience as an example for those who would believe in Him and receive eternal life.

When I found this scripture—first of all, I am quite a hardheaded person, so, I was like, *He's not talking to me*. But the apostle Paul said it, and I knew exactly who Paul was. He was a persecutor of Christians. He was mean and evil. He probably thought there was no way he ever deserved Christ's love and forgiveness either. If God loved Paul as much as He did and was willing to forgive him, surely He could do the same for me.

This scripture became like the cornerstone for the next thing I found which I call R & R: Resurrection and Redemption. Those were the two most fabulous words I ever heard in my life, especially redemption. At that time in my life I could not tell you what that word meant, so I looked it up and it said, "to bring back to a useful purpose." At that time in my life, I did not even know who I was when I looked at myself in the mirror, so redemption sounded awesome!

Redemption will bring me back to exactly what *He* chose for me. And I figured, considering the type of man Paul was, and the love, forgiveness, grace, and mercy he found in Jesus Christ—well, I surely could receive that. He promised that once I left everything behind—the bad habits, the [wrong] way of life, the things that were hurting me and constantly hurting Him, as well as hurting the people that I love; when I chose to leave those things and to die to them, He would make sure I received every benefit possible through redemption—because He chose to die and was resurrected for just that *reason*!!!

With every communion I am reminded to leave it in the past, don't even look back, don't long for anything that once belonged to the dead me because I have been redeemed and resurrected through the covenant of His death and resurrection provided for me. And I'm truly thankful for that, not only at communion but every single day.

As for that scripture, He wrote it for this hardheaded little girl.

I'm Deborah. I'm an Overcomer.

My Priority Is to Respond
Lael Barker and Susan Hill, May 4, 2013

Lael: Jesus invited us to eat at His table. Us. Me. I did not think I was able to come to the table. I was under the impression I was unworthy. Then I came here and figured out that, yeah, you're unworthy but you're still welcome!

In Mark chapter two Jesus is walking down the road gathering people to come and eat with Him. He is gathering up sinners. He is gathering up a group of us and saying, Come eat with Me, Come follow Me. Mark 2:17 says, "It is not the healthy who need a doctor but the sick. I haven't come to call the righteous but the sinners."

He is calling us. That is me! He wants me, and you, to come and partake at this table. And He calls us to follow Him. Ya know, I'm a sinner. I'm broken and weak. But He still wants me at His table and He wants me to follow Him.

So what do you need to bring to the table? Do you need to bring something so you can leave it there? To set your priorities in line? I know I do. What do you want to come to the table and pick up and take with you?

We come to this table in remembrance of Him, the bread in remembrance of His body which was broken for us. And the juice in remembrance of His blood that was shed and spilt for us.

Susan: I Corinthians 11:23- 26 says,

> For I received from the Lord what I also passed on to you: The Lord Jesus, on the night He was betrayed, took bread, and when He had given thanks, He broke it and said, "This is My body, which

is for you; do this in remembrance of Me." In the same way, after supper He took the cup, saying, "This cup is the new covenant in My blood; do this, whenever you drink it, in remembrance of Me."

For whenever you eat this bread and drink this cup, you proclaim the Lord's death until He comes.

The new covenant is a reminder of Christ's life and death, full and final payment for our sins. God invites us and our job is to respond. My priority is to respond to God's love for me which is His free gift of grace.

HOME IS WHERE YOUR HEART IS
Pat Widhalm, May 18, 2013

Hi. I'm Pat, and I'm an Overcomer.

Tonight is a special night for us being our seventh Sereniversary. I'd like to say to you all, Welcome home. If this is the first time you have been with us, we want to especially welcome you and invite you into our family. We have opened our hearts to you and hope you will do the same to us. You see, home is where your heart is!

Most of you may not be aware of this about me but I was born with a congenital heart defect. I did not even know I had it until I was diagnosed in my late 30's. Even knowing it, though, I did not consider it since it did not seem to affect me in any way. But, as we know around here, defects have a way of catching up to you; and in this last decade of my life, mine seems to be doing just that.

I was first referred to a cardiologist in 2005, and since 2009 he has been monitoring me every year. One of the things he does is an echocardiogram (like a baby sonogram for pregnant women except I'm not pregnant and my heart—well, I guess that would be my baby). During the echocardiogram he looks deep inside my heart, where you can't see, and measures how far the defect has progressed.

My heart condition has become quite a motivator for me and I have become much more heart-healthy conscious. I work very hard to stay fit and trim, vigorously exercising every day, eating healthy and watching my weight (and contrary to a popular myth about me, I can't just eat whatever I want to and not gain weight. I really do have to work at it). I hate feeling helpless to change my circumstances, and my goal with all of that has been to try and turn things around with my heart and to fix the problem myself. All the stuff I do is good for me, and I have to believe it helps, but as far as fixing my problem it has not worked.

Each year, when I get my test results, my heart problem is a little worse than it was the year before. My cardiologist is telling me now that soon I will need to submit myself to a surgeon to have an operation to correct my defect. If any of you know me, you know I don't handle operations well. In fact, they scare me. I literally have nightmares leading up to them. But no one is going to force me to have that operation. Well, Linda might; but even without Linda fussing over me, when the time comes I'm going to have that operation because if I don't my heart will fail and I will die.

In a sense, I am going to die whether I have the surgery or not. You see, when the surgeon opens my chest, he will stop my heart so he can open it up to repair the defect. In the sense that my heart won't be beating, I will be dead. I have no guarantee of the outcome. I have to trust the surgeon, that he can sustain me through death, that he has the skill to fix my heart problem, and that he can then resurrect me to new life with a renewed heart. I will choose that guy very carefully. I hope what I shared with you sounds a little familiar because I intended it to be allegorical.

Now I'd like you to consider my experience from a different perspective. Many of you may not be aware of this about yourself but from a spiritual perspective we are all born with a congenital heart defect much worse than mine. Some of you may not have gotten the diagnosis yet, some of you have but aren't concerned because you don't yet see any of the bad effects it has on your life, and some of you are well aware of your heart condition and are trying desperately to fix your heart problem yourself. I'm sure what you are doing is good but it won't work. You can't fix yourself.

All of us need an operation. If you don't get it, you will die! It is offered to you free of charge, but no one is going to force you. It is a choice you have to make.

You need Jesus. He is the only surgeon who can perform the operation you need. And the cool part is, as Pastor John has been telling us, Jesus will give you His Spirit who guarantees the outcome. You won't have to die—Jesus already did that for you, too!

That is what we are celebrating here tonight with this communion meal. Jesus went through a living nightmare and died to set us free from death so that even though our bodies may die—if you have chosen

Him and accepted what He has done for you—you have already been resurrected to a new life with a renewed heart. That is the ultimate gift of Love and the greatest reason for a celebration!

You are all invited to be a part of the celebration—both in this representative meal and in the Great Feast when Jesus returns. It is Jesus, Himself, who extends that invitation to you. As you come forward, think about what you just heard; and when you receive the bread in your hand representing His body broken for you, and dip it into the juice representing His blood shed for you, recommit yourself to Jesus (or commit yourself for the first time) and then leave your heart there in His hands. After all, home is where your heart is! Welcome home!

You Are Not Defined by the World Anymore
Aunt Laurie, March 1, 2014

We come to the Lord's table every week and, I don't know about you, but I need that. I need to present myself at this table so I remember where my true identity lies. I need to present myself to this table to remember how I'm defined. I need to present myself to this table to remember where I take my stand.

Maybe this week I found myself identifying with my biological family heritage: the angry Irish, the penny-pinching Scottish, or the abused Choctaw. What is my true Identity? Jesus said:

> I tell you, love your enemies. Help and give without expecting a return. You'll never—I promise—regret it. Live out this God-created identity the way our Father lives toward us, generously and graciously, even when we're at our worst. Our Father is kind; you be kind (Luke 6:35-36 *The Message*).

I come to this table to remind me how I'm defined. In John 17 I learned I'm not defined by the world any more than Christ is defined by the world. The world may define and divide us into: Hatfields/McCoys, kicker/rapper, black/white, this orientation/that orientation, Baptist, Methodist, Episcopalian, Sooner, Cowboy, or Aggie. *All of these are temporal, not eternal.*

The eternal truth is this:

> From now on everyone is defined by Christ, everyone is included in Christ (Colossians 3:11 *The Message*).

Where do you want to take your stand? Are you taking a stand on temporal or the eternal? I choose to take my stand at this table, where God proved His great love for us by the death of His Anointed One (Romans 5:8).

I Corinthians 15:58 says,

> With all this going for us, my dear, dear friends, stand your ground. And don't hold back. Throw yourselves into the work of the Master, confident that nothing you do for Him is a waste of time or effort (*The Message*).

I'm Aunt Laurie. I welcome you to this table.

Remember Me
Linda Widhalm, April 19, 2014—Easter

Hi. My name is Linda, and I'm an Overcomer. We are in the middle of Passover Week. The Passover was commanded by God to His people for the purpose of remembering and celebrating the salvation of their people from the death angel and their deliverance out of slavery. It was also a time to look ahead with hope to God's promise of the coming Messiah who would also save and deliver.

God knows if we remember what He did for us in the past it will help us have faith in His promises for the future. This meal is a part of the Passover meal. One of the last things Jesus did with His disciples was share the Passover meal with them. This was likely the third Passover meal He shared with them since He called them to follow Him. Luke tells us,

> And He [Jesus] took bread, gave thanks and broke it, and gave it to them, saying, "This is My body given for you; do this in remembrance of Me" (Luke 26:19).

"Do this in remembrance of Me." Those are very familiar words to us. But not for the disciples who were accustomed to this meal and all its components representing a time and events in the history of their people. Now Jesus instructed them, from here on remember Him when they ate the bread. Wow! A pivotal moment. He was saying, Your hopes, the hopes of God's chosen people, are being fulfilled!

He changed a tradition that was thousands of years old and had been commanded by God to be carried out in a specific way, at a specific time, for a specific reason, with specific consequences if not obeyed precisely. Jesus, God's Son, was giving a new command. From this day forward, "Do this in remembrance of *Me*."

Jesus only highlighted the unleavened bread and the cup:

> "This is My body given for you; ... This cup is the new covenant in My blood, which is poured out for you" (Luke 22:19, 20).

So before He was taken into custody; before He spent the night in a cold, deep, dark pit; before He was beaten, ridiculed, spat upon; before He had parts of His beard ripped out; before He stumbled down the road carrying a heavy beam through the mocking crowd; before He was nailed onto the cross, raised up, rejected by man and God; before He struggled for each breath for hours; before He died, Jesus made a decision. Before the suffering came, He changed the course of history with His words, then followed through with His actions.

My example is He. How pivotal, how tradition-changing, how fulfilling, how hope-filled this sacred moment is for each of us, individually. How fitting for us to stop remembering former things and begin, instead, to remember Him.

I'm Linda, welcoming you to come remember Him.

THE WEDDING FEAST
Breila Joy Wehrmann, May 31, 2014

[The wedding march began and Breila entered wearing her original wedding attire, complete with veil and tiara, on the arm of her father who was dressed in suit and tie.]

I'm an Overcomer. While I can't say I have walked through the Steps in order, I have experienced the fruit that each one of them brings forth. This month I celebrate 24 years of recovery from myself.

My first Step Three experience happened when I was 10 years old. For as long as I can remember, I knew and believed in the power greater than myself, Jesus Christ. I had heard all of the Bible stories, confessed my sins, and put my faith in God long before age 10. But on May 16, 1990, while sitting in a church service, God pointed out to me that those things were not enough. Until then, I had accepted Him as I understood Him. Upon understanding that He wanted more, I made the decision to turn my will and my life over to His care. This was more than believing in His sacrifice and confessing my sins to my Savior. This was truly letting Him be my Lord. This covenant I made with God that day is mirrored in the Bible by the marriage covenant, a perfect illustration of who we are to Him, His bride.

Exactly nine years later, on May 16, I married my husband, right in the middle of our church service on a Sunday morning. I could think of no better date for my wedding than the anniversary of my covenant with God as His eternal Bride. My husband and I shared communion with our church family and signed a marriage covenant. Then we shared a reception meal and celebration, complete with music, dancing, and cake.

And that is what communion means to me. It is not just a table at which we are welcome. It is a wedding feast at which we are the bride. The Body and the Blood are broken and poured out so that His covenant with us can be fulfilled. Communion happens for me every time I share a meal with family, say a prayer of thanksgiving to my Lord, put something difficult in His hands, take a step in freedom, or call out His name and claim His promises. You are all welcome at His table, but more than that, you are the reason this meal was prepared. You are His covenant Bride.

I know that some of you feel like this is something you could never attain or deserve, but I want you to know that you don't need a dress, or a crown on your head, or a perfect life to make you worthy. This communion meal is here to remind you that it is His sacrifice that makes you worthy.

If you haven't given your life over to the care of God, walk down this aisle in a few moments, receive the cleansing sacrifice of His body and His blood, and say "I do" to the One who seeks after you as His bride.

It Is for Freedom Christ Has Set Us Free
Emily Joy Kelley, age 14, December 13, 2014

Hello, Everyone. My name is Emily, and I'm an Overcomer.

I got nervous when I was asked to give the communion meditation two weeks ago. You see, speaking in front of people is not my favorite thing to do. I haven't given a communion mediation in six years, and I was not expecting to give one now. So, when I was asked, I answered with an, "I'll pray about it." Pray about it actually means repeatedly asking God, "Please don't make me do it!"

When He answered me, I tried to pretend I did not know what He was saying. After a few minutes of red, hot, flaming conviction, I said

"Okay" and surrendered to give the communion meditation. Then the pain in my chest went away and I started to feel good because the conviction-feeling was gone. I then began to freak out because I had no clue what I was supposed to say! I'm really skilled in the art of freaking out. I prayed, "God, I hope You have the communion meditation, 'cause I got nothin'!" He did not answer me right away. I knew He would eventually. I just hoped it would be before December 13th.

A few days later, my MiMi came to me with a verse. She said, "I was praying for you and this is what God showed me: Galatians 5:1."

> It is for freedom that Christ has set us free. Stand firm, then, and do not let yourselves be burdened again by a yoke of slavery.

Okay, great. Awesome verse! But what does it mean?

A few more days of asking God and His answers slowly appeared. Originally, I was focusing more on this [point to bread and juice]. And when you focus more on this [point to bread and juice], you start to focus on the rules.

Every church has different regulations for this moment. I was getting very caught up in the rules when He opened my eyes. If we let the rules get in the way of communion, Christ's death is of no value to us because He died so we could be set free of the rules. There is nothing I can do to be worthy enough for communion; but He still wants us, unworthy folk, to remember Him. He loved me so much that He died so even I could be welcomed to share this moment.

God had to teach me that this [point to bread and juice] is not communion. This [point to heart then up to God] is communion. Communion is remembering what God has done for us, what He is going to do, and what He is doing right now. This is a moment He created for us to remember what He has done for us—personally, and as a whole [gesture to everyone].

These are the four things God taught me when it comes to communion:
I'm unworthy,
I'm a sinner,
I'm *really* not perfect,
I'm welcome.

I'm Emily. Thank you for listening.

A Call to Remembrance
Hope Hightower, age 15, January 31, 2015

I am not much of a writer, lo and behold,
Here's a piece of truth I've never told.
We were all put on this earth for some reason unknown,
Or maybe the human race can't figure it out all alone.
Evolution itself is a strange weird mystery,
But I bet we could figure it out if we take a look into our history.
In a big, brown book labeled The Bible,
It tells the story of the human's survival.
Stories so strange and unexplainable,
But I bet if you read deeper, your life will be unchangeable.
One story stuck out, by far the best,
About a man in the sky putting His son to rest.

"For God so loved the world, He gave his only son,"
To be killed and crucified—way worse than shot from a gun.
He did say one thing before being killed on a tree.
He asked us to "Do this in remembrance of Me."
This story hit home and I couldn't figure out why
But maybe the truth lays with all the lies.
When Jesus was sent, it wasn't an act of heroism or bravery.
It was an act of love to end all slavery.
The Devil had us in a headlock, a grip so tight,
But Jesus came along to put up a fight.
Satan had us sinning left and right,
And the only true punishment is death on the cross
   from morning till night.

We should all die for what we have done,
But instead Jesus died for all of His loved ones.
The night at the table wasn't a "Remember My life,"
It was a "Remember My sacrifice," for all who should've died.
So instead of sitting here and listening to me,
We should all grant His one last wish:
   "Do this in Remembrance of Me."

Shame, Guilt, Humiliation, and Contempt Don't Make Miracles
Laurie Jo Gorrell, March 2015

Around Serenity Church I'm known as Aunt Laurie and I'm an Overcomer.

Is there anyone here who has ever repeatedly done something you were ashamed of and wished you had not done? Was there someone in your life who tried to pile more shame on you to make you stop? Did all that shame-piling work to make you stop?

When I was about 8 years old I began suffering from nocturnal enuresis. Does anyone know what that is? Yes, wetting the bed. My care-givers thought the best way to make me stop was to humiliate me by making me wash my sheets in a wash tub in the back yard every morning before school and hang them on a line so everyone in the neighborhood would know I wet the bed. I'd run home as fast as I could every day to try to get the sheets down, hoping none of my school friends would notice.

When I still wet the bed, even with all that shame and humiliation, I was not allowed to have sheets any more; I had to sleep on a plastic tarp. It is physically uncomfortable to sleep on plastic, but it is emotionally devastating to know the plastic is intended to shame and humiliate. I prayed every night for God to keep me from wetting the bed. I fell asleep in crackling, sweaty shame, and woke up in disappointment. I could not stop. I had no control. It was not possible for me to manage at all. But I was made to feel like the right combination of punishment, shame, and effort would produce the miracle of staying dry.

Has punishment and shame and effort ever produced a miracle for anyone in this room? Then why is that the first thing we try: with ourselves, other people, and, heaven forbid, our children?

This table is to remind me of the *new solution* for the things I'm ashamed of. Christ doesn't say, "Look what you've done!" He says, "Remember Me!" We do not approach this table in shame. We come to this table remembering that His supernatural power is exactly what I need!

What happened with my nocturnal enuresis? We moved in with my grandma, Dixie. Her approach was different. Instead of shame and punishment she used a rubber pad to protect the mattress that I never knew was there. She did for me what I could not do for myself. She gently awakened me every night and walked me to the bathroom with her arm around my shoulder, whispering kindness and love. If

. have an accident, I'd come home from school to clean sheets and ,amas and not a word of condemnation. Within a few months I had copped wetting the bed.

This is not a table to remember where I have failed but to remember He has done for me what I can't do for myself. He is there to put His arm around my shoulder and walk me through the darkest times, whispering kindness and love in my ear, giving me a clean sheet every day, and gently taking me to victory.

Shame, guilt, humiliation, and contempt don't make miracles. He does. Come to this table remembering Him, and find your miracle.

SACRED MOMENTS
Linda Widhalm, April 4, 2015

My name is Linda. I'm an Overcomer. Tonight, I want to talk to you about Sacred Moments.

Sacred Moments are those times in our lives when we become vividly aware of and partake in some aspect of the character of God and His provision in communion with Him. For me, some of those have been:

SALVATION When I was about 8 years old I came to understand for the first time that God had provided for me through the sacrifice of His only Son, Jesus, forgiveness of sin, and through His resurrection, new life. Although I did not know the meaning of the words at the time, I was enveloped in the joy of His mercy and grace through accepting His forgiveness of my sins.

Some other sacred moments followed soon after the **CONFESSION OF MY NEW FAITH** to others, **BELIEVER'S BAPTISM**, taking **HOLY COMMUNION** for the first time. All of these moments reinforced His mercy, grace, and forgiveness and filled me with His love, peace, and a sense of belonging to God and His family.

Some years later I fell in love. My **WEDDING DAY** was a sacred moment. It was a new glimpse into the unimaginable love God has for us. The giving and receiving of wedding vows are parallel to the commitment God makes to us and wants us to make to Him. As we were surrounded by friends and family, I'm sure many were renewing such commitments in their hearts as well.

The process of **BECOMING A MOTHER** was a sacred moment in my life. Each day, as my love for my child grew, I was more and more aware of what God's unconditional love really is. During those months, I made new confessions to God, accepting His will no matter the outcome, and receiving His assurance that He was with me and would remain with me. I realized the child in my womb was really His and gave her to Him. I felt like a very wealthy woman. So blessed. So cherished.

Some never experience these exact sacred moments, but that doesn't limit God's ability to reveal these same characteristics of Himself to them in other sacred moments. Likewise, some have passed through these same milestones in their lives with no thought of God. What makes any moment sacred is your awareness of God and who He is in the moment.

There have been many other sacred moments in my life, but the first sacred moment I remember in my life was when I was seven years old. It was night. I was all alone and scared in a hospital bed. The noise of New York City filtered in through the sooty window. I felt so alone. My bed, my home, my family were literally in another state. I tried to sleep but inside of me there was a growing anxiety in my chest. The weight of it began to make it difficult to breath. I sat up, put my pillow in my lap, folded my arms across my stomach, and began to rock back and forth. As the feelings inside of me continued to grow, I tried to figure out what was wrong with me and what would make it stop. I had never felt this way before. Finally, within myself—not out loud, I yelled, "I need someone to pray for me!"

Getting my feelings into words and expressing them made me feel a little less pressurized but next tears were threatening. Suddenly, a gentle voice seemed to come from within me. It said, "You can talk to Me yourself."

I looked around wondering where that voice had come from. But, well, what He said seemed so reasonable to me. So I said, again within myself, "God, I'm scared about the surgery tomorrow. Please take care of me." Peace flooded in and anxiety drained away. Soon, I laid back down, amazed and happy that God had talked to me. He listened to my prayer. And He helped me feel better. I slept.

A moment like what happened in that hospital bed does not happen very often in a person's life, but this moment we are about to share in is very special because it doesn't happen only once in a lifetime; it is not for only one, two, or a few people. It is for everyone. Everyone has the opportunity in this moment together to let it be sacred by remembering Jesus and being thankful to God and Jesus Christ for the great sacrifice and work of redemption represented here; or maybe by yielding to the work of the Holy Spirit in your heart; to accept God's forgiveness for your sins; to join God in forgiving yourself for your shortcomings; to join in God's work by forgiving someone else for wrongs they have done to you; or by allowing the Holy Spirit to meet whatever need you have in your heart.

Please bow your heads for a few moments of reflection while the servers are served.

A LIVING SAVIOR WHO IS CRAZY-IN-LOVE WITH US
Pam De Santiago, April 11, 2015

Hi. I'm Pam. I'm an Overcomer.

The thoughts I'm sharing tonight aren't what I had originally planned. Yesterday, God allowed me to get a different perspective on communion.

Yesterday afternoon my daughter and I were driving behind a car that struck and badly injured a pedestrian. In a moment, the things on my "to do" list changed to things I can't un-see.

As I tried to write down the words I wanted to say tonight regarding communion, my mind kept returning to a broken body and blood pouring out. I have heard it, I have said it, but until yesterday I had never seen it. That changed everything for me.

That young woman was in the wrong place at the wrong time and was injured by no fault of anyone. Jesus was in the right place, at the right time, and knew what to expect.

I believe the picture in my mind will change if I ever have the opportunity to meet that young woman face to face and see her as healed and whole. Jesus said, "Do this in remembrance of Me," not that He would forever be an image of a broken man on a cross but that He is a Living Savior who is crazy-in-love with us.

I tell you my thoughts tonight because there is healing in sharing with people you love and trust. If you have something in your life that hurts, that you are having trouble wishing away, the great news is you are in the right place at the right time. God would like to hear from you and would like for you to come and receive the gift that He willingly gave us: the body of Christ, broken for you. The blood of Christ poured out for you.

Extravagant Measures to Be with You
Jessica Kelley, August 15, 2015

Hi. I'm Jessica, and I'm an Overcomer.

I want to tell you about my eighth wedding anniversary. Jason did not tell me what we were going to do, he just told me I needed to put on my nicest outfit and be ready by five o'clock.

This was exciting and scary all at the same time. I was really excited to see what he had in store for us but, for someone who probably has some OCD, not knowing the plan can be disconcerting. What if I didn't have the right outfit on? Would my nicest outfit be good enough? What if I'm overdressed? But, once I got ready, Jason told me I looked great and was perfectly dressed for the occasion. I realized I was going to have to trust him.

We pulled up to a very nice looking restaurant and stopped at the valet stand. As the nice man opened my door for me, I was instantly aware of the fact the we drove an old minivan, and that ours probably did not fit in with the type of vehicles he was used to parking. But Jason came around and took my hand. His face was so full of excitement that I was able to let those concerned feelings go and head into the restaurant.

The hostess greeted us warmly and asked if we had a reservation. Jason told her we were the Kelleys and she said, "Welcome! Happy anniversary!" She took us right to our table, and the waiter pulled out my chair for me to sit down then gently put my napkin across my lap. It did not take long for me to realize that I was not dressed elegantly enough for this restaurant, even if Jason thought so. But the staff did not let on that they noticed, and they continued to serve us as if we were just as important and special as all the other guests they had that evening. The whole dinner was amazing, even the water tasted better than I have ever tasted!

When we were through eating, we had food left over. I really wanted to take it home with me but was not sure if it was proper etiquette at a place like this to ask for a to-go box. Our waiter must have read my mind because he asked me if I'd like him to box up our meal. That was the most beautiful To Go box I have ever seen. The food was garnished again, wrapped in silver wrapping, and placed in a pretty, silver gift bag. When the meal was over, the waiter helped me out of my chair, told us both it was a pleasure to serve us and that he hoped we had a very happy anniversary.

That dinner was probably the best food I ever ate. Our mouths still water when we think of the food we ate that night, but that was not the best part of the evening. My favorite part of that date was something Jason said right after we sat down at the table. Jason told me that he wanted to take me there because he wanted to not only tell me but to show me how much he loved me and how important I was to him. He wanted to take me somewhere extravagant because that is how special I am to him.

When we come to the communion table, I think that is what God is saying to us. He is inviting us to come spend time with Him because He wants to remind us how much He loves us. He wants us to remember the extravagant thing He did for us because He loves us so much.

Sometimes we look at ourselves and we feel uncomfortable because of things that we have done, or not done, and we are worried about what God or other people are thinking about us. But God is right there saying to us, "I'm inviting you here because I love you and I want to spend time with you. You are special to Me, and I will go to extravagant measures to be with you."

THE GIRL STANDING HERE
Mercy Wehrmann, October 17, 2015

Hi! I'm Mercy, and I'm eleven.

I wrote a poem about what Communion means to me and it is called, "The Girl Standing Here."

> I've made a new friend. He's really great.
> He sits by my side every time I pray.
> In the battle of evil, hate, and despair—a tear from my eye.
> As I fall on my knees, Jesus hears my cry.
> I sit at my table crying my tears,
> The Bible is open, Psalm 46 eases my fears.
> Many are saying, "Who can show us any good?"
> Let the light of Your Presence shine on us, Lord, if you could.
> The people in heaven will love Him forever.
> The girl standing here will doubt Him never.
> Your beauty, Your love, Your compassion and grace,
> You touch my hand and I'm painless in Your embrace.

Thank you.

Don't Miss the Grace of God
David Redding, March 25, 2013

Hello, I'm David.

"See to it," the writer of Hebrews tells us, "that no one misses the grace of God" (Hebrews 12:15a). I don't know about you, but I have missed a lot of things in my life. In fact, one of the most traumatic experiences I can remember in my childhood was missing the school bus. I can't shake that totally helpless feeling of running toward the bus stop, screaming at the top of my lungs and waving my I-Dream-of-Jeannie lunch box frantically in the air, all the while watching the back of the bus fade away into the distance. It was devastating.

As fallen humans, we are, among other things, a sorry lot of miss-ers. We miss phone calls, we miss appointments, and we all have suffered that miserable feeling of missing our turn or exit. More importantly, we miss opportunities. We miss the point. And we miss the proverbial mark time and time again. But the one thing we are exhorted not to miss is the grace of God.

Yet for much of my life I missed it badly, not because I was chasing after it, screaming, arms flailing wildly, and just could not catch up with it, but because I simply did not realize I needed it.

Isn't it great news to know that our God comes after us? Of all the stories in the Bible of God pursuing us with His grace, perhaps the most meaningful to me is found in John 8. Jesus was teaching an early morning Bible class in the temple when suddenly a group of religious leaders barged in dragging a woman who they claimed was caught in the act of adultery. She had no way out. She knew it. They all knew it; that is why they already had stones in hands. So they said to Jesus,

> Teacher, this woman was caught in the act of adultery. In the law, Moses commanded us to stone such women. Now what do you say? (John 8:4-5)

But Jesus bent down and started to write on the ground with His finger. When they kept on questioning Him, He stood up and said something to this effect, "Alright, go ahead and *stone* her. But let the one of you without sin throw the first stone." He then again stooped down and wrote on the ground.

You know, that is just like Jesus. He is willing to stoop. He stooped when He washed the feet of the disciples and when He pulled Peter up from sinking into the sea. He stooped to pray, and again He stooped to pick up His cross. Here, He stooped to write in the dust. Have you ever wondered what He wrote in that dust? You would not be the first. Many have speculated.

Some believe He began composing a list of the sins of the accusers. That makes sense because of what happened next. Do you remember? Listen! Stones began dropping to the ground and the accusers began leaving one by one until only Jesus and the woman remained. Can you imagine her thinking "What just happened?" Something had happened. Grace happened. Something Jesus would not allow her to miss. Something we are told not to miss.

God's grace comes running after us like a tigress snatching up her cub by the nape of the neck to save it from disaster. I don't think this woman totally understood it, but she also did not miss it. She was saved from disaster through grace.

When Jesus stooped down to write in the dust that morning—and I really have no way of knowing—here's what I believe he wrote:

"Grace happened here!"

Which brings us around the table tonight. It is stinking awesome that we don't have to run after Him, screaming with arms flailing, in an attempt to get His attention. *He* comes after *us*, then He stoops to our level and offers all of Himself—His body, His blood, His Spirit.

Grace was His idea. His best idea. And it happens here.

Let's not miss it.

Section 2

OVERCOMERS

Jesus Christ, our Higher Power

We've spent enough time
cleaning up cobwebs.

It's time to do something
about the spider!

- adapted from a
time-worn sermon illustration

Overcomers Preamble

Hi. I'm _____, and I'm an Overcomer

Overcomers is a fellowship of men and women who have been affected either directly or indirectly by something destructive that is out of our control. We believe that as we look to a loving God for help and put into practice those principles for living which He has given us in His Word, we will find both the strength and the freedom we need to live productive and happy lives. We strongly believe that our "Higher Power" is Jesus Christ.

Our five-fold purpose, based directly upon the Word of God, is set forth as follows:

1. To provide fellowship and recovery
2. To be and to live reconciled to God and His family
3. To gain a better understanding of our problems
4. To be built up and strengthened in our faith in Christ
5. To give dedicated service to others who are suffering as we once suffered

We practice the suggested 12 Step Recovery Program because we believe these to be the practical application of the life-changing principles clearly set forth in Scripture. We welcome anyone who has a desire to recover from their pain, anyone who has a desire to rise above the pain and turmoil brought into their lives by a loved one, anyone who is not opposed to our general method of recovery. We are here to share our experience, strength, and hope with one another. The loving support and genuine care of fellow members, coupled with daily prayer and the reading of Scripture, prepares us to experience total serenity in Christ, no matter what our outward circumstances might be.

Attendance at additional 12 Step groups is encouraged. We are dedicated to the principles of anonymity and confidentiality. We guard the anonymity and confidences of other members without compromise. Nothing said in these discussions will leave this room in any form. Gossip has no place among us. We will share nothing said in this room with anybody outside this group. Our common welfare must come first.

There is only one authority in our group: Jesus Christ, as He expresses His love and healing among us.

I'm _____. Thanks for letting me serve.

How to Conduct an Overcomers Meeting

After reading the Overcomers Preamble (page 59) you should have some idea what Overcomers is. Our Overcomers Fellowship is a 12 Step group exactly like home groups and fellowships which so many of us come from—with two major exceptions.

We acknowledge Jesus Christ as the Higher Power in our group and everyone is welcome. Overcomers is for everyone because everyone has something in their lives that has hurt them, or something out of their control they cannot will or wish away. Overcomers needs everyone because everyone has something to share which someone else needs to hear.

The following pages present readings essential to conducting an Overcomers meeting, then come examples of Overcomers Topics to get the meeting started; some relate to coins of the month, some are based on a Step or an excerpt from *The Big Book of Alcoholics Anonymous* or an AA slogan, while others are based on a topic relevant to the group or leader.

The topics are followed by actual shares given during a meeting as a result of the given topic. Everything said in Overcomers is confidential, so all of the personal stories, from topic introductions to shares, were shared by their authors for publication in this book—for you.

TAKING THE FLOOR

Every person that speaks at the meeting introduces themself before saying what they want to say or reading what they want to read, and gives the group a chance to respond back even if they have already spoken before. Example:

Hi. My name is Linda, and I'm an Overcomer.

Group in unison: "Hi, Linda!"

Each time a speaker finishes, the group responds by thanking them.

Group in unison: "Thanks, Linda!"

This pattern should be familiar to previous attenders of 12 Step groups. Opening in this way helps people to not only remember each others' names but gives respect to the speaker, draws wandering minds back to the group, and provides an easy way for the leader to regain the floor when needed.

Readings

You will need to make copies of the following readings so they can be passed out during your meeting to those individuals who have been asked to read. The readings can be printed from our website, http:// SerenityChurch.net. In the left column click on PDF Downloads. We laminate ours. You can also find banners and posters of The 12 Steps, The 12 Promises, The Serenity Prayer, and The Lord's Prayer elsewhere on-line; these can be helpful to newcomers. Be sure your version of The Lord's Prayer is the same as the one found later in this book.

Let me say here, good reading abilities are not necessary when choosing a reader. It is essential that patience and help be given to the one who struggles to read; after all, reading issues may be a basis of many people's struggles with addiction. Overcomers is about overcoming *every*thing that hinders.

The readings will be familiar, to a degree, to anyone who has previously attended any type of 12 Step group. The readings provide information, continuity, group participation, and comfort.

Overcomers Leader Format (page 69) The leader takes the floor and begins guiding the group through the starred items. Next, the leader reads the "Intro to Sharing" before presenting a topic. Guiding the Group to Take a Collection and To End the Meeting are also included.

The Overcomers Preamble (page 59) This preamble is unique to Overcomers and sets both the purpose and a few guidelines. This is read by a volunteer chosen before the meeting.

How it Works (page 71)) The 12 Steps is adapted from *The Big Book of Alcoholics Anonymous*, pages 58-60, for use in Overcomers meetings. This is read by a volunteer chosen before the meeting. (Some groups only read half of page 60.)

The 12 Promises (page 74) - This is adapted from *The Big Book of Alcoholics Anonymous*, page 83, and is read by a volunteer chosen before the meeting.

Presentation of Coins (page 72) This reading is unique to Overcomers and is performed by a seasoned volunteer chosen before the meeting.

Sponsorship (page 73) When our meetings were smaller we did not routinely mention sponsorship. When the need became apparent we added this reading to every meeting. It may not be appropriate for your group at every meeting.

COINS, MEDALLIONS, CHIPS

Whichever word you prefer (we use them all), coins are another familiar connection to other 12 Step groups. Coins provide a welcome, a point of celebration, a tangible reminder, and a feeling of inclusion.

We start by welcoming newcomers by offering them a Never Alone Again chip. We ask those who are new to stand up and say their name. Then the "Magnificent Mistress of Medallions" or the "Chipper Chip Chap" hugs them and gives them the coin. Like we say, "Nothing is free at Overcomers. Everything costs a hug."

Obviously coins cost money, and it could take some time for a new group to afford these coins. I have sent a page of paper coins to prison inmates to tear apart and use at meetings; paper coins only have a coin's words on them. Be creative. We try to have a new coin each month.

But you could just as easily focus on a recovery slogan without having a coin. The most important thing is the welcome and the message that the newcomer Never has to Be Alone Again.

We collect coins leftover at the end of the month to use in a Grab-Bag meeting where everyone pulls out a coin and shares on the topic stated on the coin. These make for very interesting meetings!

The Serenity Coin (not actually used in Overcomers) We purchase our coins from Wendell's; their information is easily found online. We offer to any Serenity Church the opportunity to use the coin we minted at Wendell's which bears our logo on front and the Serenity Prayer on back. We put our Serenity coins in a welcome bag which is offered to any first-time visitors to Serenity Church. We also carry a coin with us to give to people we encounter in our daily life, handed out much like a business card. This coin has our web address on it, but Wendell's can customize it for your web address.

WELCOME KIT

(Presentation of Welcome Kit, page 73) As newcomers introduce themselves, a volunteer is ready with pen in hand to write the newcomer's name on something that will be given to the newcomer later.

We use an envelope that contains a few items we hope will encourage them in the days ahead. One item is an Overcomers Brochure* which contains all the readings used in the meetings. This brochure can be used during a meeting instead of laminated copies. The next item is another brochure: Why Do I Need a Sponsor?*

But the main purpose for the Welcome Kit is phone numbers. We pass envelopes around the room to all attendees except the newcomers; attendees list their first name and phone number on the outside of the envelope. Men write on envelopes for men; women on envelopes for women. Not all attendees are comfortable giving their information and it is not required. This is, however, a Step 12 opportunity.

At the end of the meeting, the leader or other designated person explains that those in the group who wrote their names and numbers did so with the expectation they be used. Also included is a mention that "You never have to be alone again in your struggles. Use the number so you don't use." The leader then gives the appropriate envelope to each newcomer with, of course, another hug. Now the group has provided the newcomer with two of the eight hugs some experts say we need per day.

We tried pre-printing names and phone numbers on the envelopes in an effort to be less distracting during meetings but abandoned the practice because the newcomer needs the names of those actually at the meeting which they attended. It does not hurt for them to see our love in action if they notice it being done.

SIZE OF GROUP AND LOCATION

It only takes two people to start a group. The first-ever Overcomers group had only two people for a very long time—years. We have had groups of over 50 on Birthday Night or other special occasions. It is not the size of the group that matters but the desire of those involved to get better and provide experience, strength, and hope to others wanting to get better.

We usually arrange chairs in a circle. It is better to not have too many chairs. Add more as they are needed.

We offer Overcomers several nights a week by partnering with other organizations to offer Overcomers in their location. Some of these groups are more AA focused, some are more Al-Anon focused. Non-church locations can be more inviting to those who have not embraced Christ yet.

* available for download at www.serenitychurch.net

LENGTH OF MEETING

One hour. Stick to it. Prompt starts and stops are respectful, a personal trait every addict is trying both to learn and to abide by in all other areas of life.

Since the meeting starts with readings, late comers can easily slip in and join the group with little interruption. If the late arrival is a newcomer, be sure to back up and welcome them with a Never Alone Again coin when the share in progress has finished. It may also be necessary to briefly restate the topic for the night.

Old-timers will catch on to the topic by themselves. When the meeting is ended, those who need to are free to leave. Others are then free to greet the newcomers and carry on the "meeting after the meeting."

PRAYER DURING MEETINGS

In addition to every meeting beginning with The Serenity Prayer (see Leader Format, page 69) and ending with The Lord's Prayer (page 75), the leader may pause the meeting in response to someone's share in order to call on our Higher Power, Jesus Christ. The leader may pray them self, or call upon an individual whom they are sure is comfortable praying for the need expressed.

This is definitely not part of most 12 Step meetings but is what sets Overcomers apart as a group who has a name for our Higher Power: Jesus Christ. It is our tradition to say "This is our prayer. Jesus is Lord" in unison after the Amen.

We also take the opportunity, at times, to allow everyone to call out the name of someone who needs the Lord's help. After each name is called, the group responds together, "This is our prayer. Jesus is Lord," then end the sharing time with The Lord's Prayer.

TAKING UP COLLECTION, AND ANNOUNCEMENTS

We pass a basket at the end of every Overcomers meeting to pay for coins, building use, and other supplies such as coffee. This is also a good time to give announcements or make a "group conscious decision" such as whether to give someone gas money to attend a funeral. Making collections and giving announcements at the beginning can derail a meeting.

BIRTHDAY NIGHT

Birthday Night is a special time we celebrate annual increments of recovery. Ours are conducted the last Saturday of each month after our regular Serenity Church service. Even folks who attend other Overcomers meetings throughout the week will celebrate with the big group on Saturday. So far no one has arrived at their first birthday without becoming involved with Serenity Church, but it could happen with remote Overcomers groups.

The Overcomers Birthday Night meeting begins as usual through readings and giving of Never Alone Again and monthly chips—but not annual chips. The Leader announces those celebrating birthdays and the number of years they have been in recovery. Folks cheer after each announcement! Then the leader offers each celebrant time to share how they did it, how they continued to add up days of recovery. A suggested format for sharing is: What my life was like, What happened, and What my life is like now.

If there are a lot of celebrants, a time limit may be set to allow all a turn to share. When sharing is finished, and if time permits, the Leader takes the floor to say something like, "This is the one time we allow crosstalk in Overcomers (see page 70). Please feel free to encourage our celebrants."

Before the meeting ends with the Lord's Prayer, each celebrant is given their birthday chip by a significant person in their life—sponsor, spouse, child, friend, pastor, etc.

If you only have an Overcomers group and not a church yet, Birthday Night is a great time to celebrate Holy Communion together. After the celebrants have shared, read a Scripture such as 1 Corinthians 11:23-26:

> For I received from the Lord that which I also delivered to you, that the Lord Jesus on the night in which He was betrayed took bread; and when He had given thanks, He broke it and said, "This is My body, which is for you; do this in remembrance of Me."

> In the same way He took the cup also after supper, saying, "This cup is the new covenant in My blood; do this, as often as you drink it, in remembrance of Me." For as often as you eat this bread and drink the cup, you proclaim the Lord's death until He comes.

Choose two of the celebrants to serve the elements to those gathered. We take communion by dipping the bread into the juice. We let everyone stay seated as the servers move around the circle. Ask those desiring to partake to lift their palm up to receive the bread, otherwise they will be passed by. (If red flags are going off for you, here, please see Section 1: Holy Communion.) The person serving the bread will go first around the circle, offering the bread and saying something to each partaker such as, "This is His body, broken for you." The person offering the juice then follows, saying something like, "This is His blood, shed for you."

Lighting

It can be more welcoming to have subdued lighting. First-time guests may feel more comfortable, and difficult sharing is made easier. Floor lamps work well in some locations. Large rooms can be made to feel a better size by lighting only the area to be used.

Variety of Meetings

Eventually folks who have been coming for a long time may need some variety in the way things are done. We try not to get stuck in any rut for too long. Some practices we have adopted to help are:

First Meeting of the Month We focus monthly meetings on the Step of the same number as the month, so in January we focus on Step 1, and so on.

Speaker Meetings Sometimes a Seasoned Serenitarian or other Christ-follower in recovery is invited to share their experience, strength, and hope. This format is used: What my life was like, What happened, and What it is like now. It is important to not spend too much time on the first point, with most of the time spent on the second and third points.

Instead of setting up a circle, have a podium and chairs in rows. We still open and close the meeting with readings and prayers, there is simply no topic or open floor sharing during the meeting.

Fifth Wednesday of the Month is Gratitude Meeting Proceed around the circle giving everyone an opportunity to share what they are grateful for. We have done this the week of Thanksgiving, too.

We Do Not Take Off for Holidays

Holidays are the most stressful times for people in recovery. Being around relatives and tables set with alcohol are very difficult for many.

Be sure a reliable individual is available and assigned to chair the meetings around the holidays. Some of our seasoned sponsors open their homes to host a Thanksgiving meal or holiday barbeque for individuals who do not feel safe going "home."

Childcare

During weekday Overcomers Meetings we generally do not provide childcare. Folks can usually find someone to leave their children with for an hour. Also, since we meet several times a week, spouses can alternate meetings. (For more on this topic see page 147.)

Sponsors Are a Must

Recovery does not occur for anyone without a burning desire and consistent hard work. It is rarely, if ever, achieved and maintained alone. One of the ways an individual maintains their recovery is by helping others with recovery. We have found it helpful to address this issue near the close of meetings on a regular basis by saying something like,

> We believe the miracle of recovery happens when you actively participate in this program; that includes attending meetings, sharing in meetings, and working the Steps with a sponsor.

> A sponsor should be someone who has developed a mature perspective in the same area of recovery which you are struggling with. A sponsor should be someone for whom you do not and would not develop romantic feelings.

> Sometimes a temporary sponsor can give you support while you take your time to carefully choose the sponsor who guides you through the Steps.

> Can I have a show of hands of those who have worked the Steps and are willing to sponsor others? If you have not worked the Steps with the support of a sponsor, please note the lifted hands and prayerfully consider asking one of these to sponsor you on this journey.

Tissues Are a Must

That's it. Tissues are a must.

To Help Get Your Group Started

You will need copies of the readings. Examples are in this book, but more helpful are the PDF files found on our website. Go to www.serenitychurch.net and choose PDF Downloads from the left column.

Read and use the Overcomers Meetings Topic Introductions, which begin on page 77, as well as the other helpful things that have been shared in our meetings.

Overcomers Leader Format

Before the Meeting

Pick people to read the Preamble, How it Works, and the Promises. Assign someone to present chips and Welcome Kits. Be sure the chips needed are available.

To Begin the Meeting

Leader takes the floor by saying:

> Welcome everyone to the ___[Saturday night]___ meeting of Overcomers. My name is ___[John]___, and I'm an Overcomer.

Leader then says:

> Please silence your cell phones
>
> Please join me in a moment of silence followed by the Serenity Prayer:
>
>> God, grant me the serenity
>> To accept the things I cannot change,
>> Courage to change the things I can,
>> And wisdom to know the difference
>
> I've asked a friend to read the Preamble
>
> I've asked a friend to read How it Works (the 12 Steps)
>
> I've asked a friend to read the Promises
>
> I've asked a friend to hand out Chips

Leader then writes newcomer's name on the Welcome Kit and passes it around the circle with a pen.

Leader Takes the Floor to Give Intro to Sharing

> Overcomers is different from other 12 Step meetings because there are as many reasons for being here as there are people attending. We also differ from other fellowships in that we directly identify our Higher Power as Jesus Christ.
>
> While our struggles are all different, we do share the common solution of other 12 Step fellowships, found in our Steps. In order to stay focused on our common solution, we ask that while sharing you follow some simple guidelines:

Please avoid cross talk. Cross talk is defined as responding directly to another person's share by giving advice or specific personal experience. While it is our goal to share our experience, strength, and hope, we ask that, if you have something specific to say to another person, you wait until after the meeting.

Because our struggles are different, we ask that while sharing you not focus on the problem but *share on the common solution* we have found.

Please *limit your sharing to 3 to 5 minutes* to allow everyone the opportunity to share.

The Leader then suggests a meeting topic and opens the floor to sharing.

Five minutes before the end of the meeting, Leader again takes the floor and explains:

Overcomers is self-supporting, so we're going to pass a basket. Newcomers get a pass; tonight you're our guest.

While the basket is being passed, I've asked a friend to ask for willing sponsors. [Leader may use a reading instead.]

To End the Meeting

Leader nods to the person who will present the Welcome Kits, then says:

Let's stand and circle up* to end the meeting with the Lord's Prayer.

Who gives power to the powerless? Our Father....

---

* During this final prayer, we at Serenity Church link our arms around each other.

How It Works

The following is adapted from *Alcoholics Anonymous*, pp. 58-60.

Step 1: We admitted we were powerless over what hurts us, that our lives had become unmanageable.

Step 2: We came to believe that a Power greater than ourselves could restore us to sanity.

Step 3: We made a decision to turn our will and our lives over to the care of God as we understood Him.

Step 4: We made a searching and fearless moral inventory of ourselves.

Step 5: We admitted to God, to ourselves, and to another human being the exact nature of our wrongs.

Step 6: We were entirely ready to have God remove all these defects of character.

Step 7: We humbly asked Him to remove all our shortcomings.

Step 8: We made a list of all persons we had harmed and became willing to make amends to them all.

Step 9: We made direct amends to such people wherever possible, except when to do so would injure them or others.

Step 10: We continued to take personal inventory and, when we were wrong, promptly admitted it.

Step 11: We sought through prayer and meditation to improve our conscious contact with God, as we understood Him, praying only for knowledge of His will for us and the power to carry that out.

Step 12: Having had a spiritual awakening as the result of these Steps, we tried to carry this message to others and practice these principles in all our affairs.

PRESENTATION OF COINS

Hi. I'm _____, and I'm an Overcomer.

[Pause for the response, "Hi, _____!"]

At Overcomers, we believe the most important person in the room is the newcomer. We all know what it took for you to come through that door for the first time. Welcome. We have a special gift we want to give you. This is how we welcome you into our family.

Is anyone here for the first time in an Overcomers Meeting? Please stand and tell us your name.

[Repeat their name, give hug, give chip to each newcomer.]

The front side of that coin says "Never Alone Again." Carry it with you to remind you of our commitment to you, as your new family, that you never have to be alone again in your struggles.

Is there anyone coming back to us who would like another Welcome chip? Or does anyone want to begin a new journey?

[Give hug, give chip.]

We also celebrate monthly increments of recovery. Is anyone celebrating 30 days of recovery?

[Give hug, give chip.]

Two months? (*etc.*)

Is there anyone celebrating annual increments of recovery this month? How many years? [*Make a record for Birthday Night*] We look forward to celebrating with you the last Saturday night of this month.

If there is a coin of the month, read the coin then pass a bag of them around for each one to take one who does not yet have one.

To close presentation time:

I'm _____. Thanks for letting me serve.

PRESENTATION OF WELCOME KIT

Hi. I'm _____, and I'm an Overcomer.

[Pause for the response, "Hi, _____!")

Address the Newcomers by name by reading their names off the envelopes. Say:

> We have another gift for you before you leave the meeting. While everyone was sharing, your brothers and sisters in the circle tonight have written their names and phone numbers down. They did so with the expectation that it be used. You never have to be alone again in your struggles. Pick up the phone. Use the number so you don't use. Call one of us 24/7. We know the darkest times inside are when it's dark outside.

[Give them the envelope and, of course, give another hug.]

I'm _____, and I'm an Overcomer.

SPONSORSHIP

> We believe the miracle of recovery happens when you actively participate in this program—that includes attending meetings, sharing in meetings, and working the Steps with a sponsor. A sponsor should be someone who has developed a mature perspective in the same area of recovery which you are struggling with. A sponsor should be someone for whom you do not have, and for whom you would not likely develop romantic feelings. Sometimes a temporary sponsor can give you support while you take your time to carefully choose the sponsor who guides you through the Steps.

> Can I have a show of hands of those who have worked the Steps and are willing to sponsor others? If you have not worked the Steps with the support of a sponsor, please note the lifted hands and prayerfully consider asking one of these to sponsor you on this journey.

The 12 Promises
from *Alcoholics Anonymous* pg. 83

If we are pains-taking about this phase of our development, we will be amazed before we are half-way through.

1. We are going to know a new freedom and a new happiness.
2. We will not regret the past nor wish to shut the door on it.
3. We will comprehend the word serenity.
4. We will know peace.
5. No matter how far down the scale we have gone, we will see how our experience can benefit others.
6. That feeling of uselessness and self-pity will disappear.
7. We will lose interest in selfish things and gain interest in our fellows.
8. Self-seeking will slip away.
9. Our whole attitude and outlook upon life will change.
10. Fear of people and economic insecurity will leave us.
11. We will intuitively know how to handle things which used to baffle us.
12. We will suddenly realize that God is doing for us what we could not do for ourselves.

Are these extravagant promises? We think not.

They are being fulfilled among us; sometimes quickly, sometimes slowly. They will always materialize if we work for them.

I'm _____. Thanks for letting me serve.

THE LORD'S PRAYER

Leader: Who gives Power to the Powerless?

[*Alternate*: Let this circle represent what we can do together, that all of us failed to do alone, with Whose help?]

Our Father, who art in heaven,

Hallowed be Thy name.

Thy kingdom come,

Thy will be done,

On earth as it is in heaven.

Give us this day our daily bread,

And forgive us our trespasses

As we forgive those who have trespassed against us,

And lead us not into temptation

But deliver us from evil.

For Thine is the kingdom,

And the power,

And the glory

Forever and ever.

Amen.

*T*he chains of habit are too weak to be felt
until they are too strong to be broken.
Samuel Johnson

Overcomers Topic Introductions and Shares
ON THE 12 STEPS

STEP 1 MEETING
Anonymous, January 2014

Step 1: We admitted we were powerless over what hurts us,
that our lives had become unmanageable.

There is usually a specific moment in our lives that is the turning point at which we realize our power and control over a particular thing is only a delusion. Delusion is defined as a belief or impression that is not in accordance with a generally accepted reality.

Up until this specific moment, most of us can realize, looking back, that we lived our lives as illusionists—magicians or conjurers. We tried desperately to put on a false front and get other people to believe it was the real thing. In fact, it was nothing more than an illusion. Illusion is defined as a false or unreal perception or belief; a deceptive appearance or impression.

Once this moment happens, we can never again go back to our delusion, our false belief. Oh, we may keep doing the same destructive behavior, but we know it for what it is and cannot fool ourselves anymore.

For me, it was a Thursday. I remember vividly standing before my two daughters as they requested to spend the weekend with a friend. "But, your dad is coming home this weekend," I said. After exchanging a glance with each other, they said, "We know."

The veil fell from my eyes. I had only been fooling myself that I was protecting them from their father's anger, but not fooling them. Permission to go to their friend's house was granted. That weekend was the beginning of the biggest change of my life. For me, I realized that I needed help. I needed the counsel of someone who was not invested in my illusions and self delusion to help steer me to safer ground.

How about you? Will you share with the group about the first moment you realized your own powerlessness or how you came to admit your life was unmanageable by you?

Step 1 Prayer

adapted from *The Big Book of Alcoholics Anonymous*

*G*od, my name is _____. I'm powerless over _____ ...
and I need Your help today. Amen.

Step 2 Meeting
Renée Bagbey, February 2013

Step 2: We came to believe that a Power greater than ourselves could restore us to sanity.

One of the pieces of literature used in the circles of recovery defines sanity as: "Soundness of mind." Although I cannot tell you the exact day God gave me a soundness of mind, I can share the time He made me aware that He had already done so. The moment that God made me aware of this gift of peace is vividly clear in my mind. Even though I strongly suspect He had offered this to me on a number of occasions prior to this day, this one stuck with me.

I lived alone and I did not have a vehicle. I walked everywhere I went. One particular evening, it had been a long day for me and I noticed a white 8½ x 11 notice on my efficiency apartment's front door as I walked over to unlock it. As I drew closer to the door, my vision fell upon the big bold letters: "3 Days!" It was an eviction notice.

I went inside and free-fell on top of my neatly made bed, landing flat on my back. I screamed, "Why God?" as my eyes pierced through my apartment's ten-foot ceiling. I had been praying every morning and night, went to meetings (sometimes two or three a day), and called my sponsor every single day. I decided this was not fair and called my sponsor to report this. Her husband informed me she was at a women's meeting and he would give me a ride to where she was.

After the meeting, my sponsor and I went into a very small bathroom, about the size of a phone booth (for those who remember what that is) and I proceeded to tell her my sad story. As I expressed how obviously and blatantly undeserving the 3-Day notice was, she asked me the most unusual question. In the mist of all my tears streaming down my red face, as other parts of me were flailing in the air, she asked, "Renée, did you take a drink today?"

Well! In disbelief that she had even asked me that, I spouted out, "Of course not! That hasn't even crossed my mind!" With the slightest pause, a very large, peaceful smile grew on her face from ear to ear for we both knew the reality of how impossible it had been for me to even draw a sober breath just six months prior to that moment in time.

Without a word, my arms slowly came down to my sides. In the quiet of that very moment I knew how un-crazy that really was. Since there was no room to move around, we both just stood there, not saying another word. Life no longer made me drink. And now I had a smile growing on my face. The obsession that once overrode all other thoughts was simply gone. And that was the moment in time God made me realize (in the center of my whirlwind panic) that He had already prepared me for that day with the gift of "soundness of mind."

This still holds true for me today. No matter what I apply this Step to, God restores my peace in all my circumstances, which makes me want to give it all to Him every day.

STEP 2 PRAYER

from The Big Book of Alcoholics Anonymous, pg. 59

*G*od, I'm standing at the turning point right now. Give me Your protection and care as I abandon myself to You and give up my old ways and my old ideas just for today. Amen.

STEP 3 MEETING
Jennifer (Horton) Michie, March 2010

Step 3: We made a decision to turn our will and our lives over to the care of God as we understood Him.

To me Step 3 is an ongoing and progressive step. The Step states that we surrender to the care of God "as we understand Him." Our understanding of God grows as we grow. Our concept of God affects our ability to surrender. If we are having trouble surrendering, it may be that it is time to step back from "trying to surrender" and focus on understanding God.

For example, if we view God as harsh, demanding, and critical, chances are we will approach Him in a defensive, fearful way and will only offer the parts of ourselves that we feel can bear the punishment we presume is coming.

If we view Him as "loving and merciful" yet generally displeased with us because we are always letting Him down, we will approach Him timidly with guilt and shame having little hope of a better outcome.

Our surrender may be accompanied by an underlying sense of defeat because, ultimately, the change rests on me and, up to this date considering my track record, I do not have much faith in me.

The God of my childhood brought me to a certain amount of surrender. It was the type of surrender that happens when you know someone has the upper hand. My surrender was a combination of my hope for something better accompanied by fear of punishment if things kept on the way they were going.

The God of my childhood was very authoritative and had a stern face. He had a very loving side but mostly He had a very high expectation of me. I could never measure up. There was only so long I could take the trying when my efforts inevitably were destined to fail.

It was a roller coaster. I would do great for a while and feel like God was pleased with me and then the smallest thing would send me reeling because I knew that I had "done it again" and He was not happy. It was a sin-conscious, performance-based relationship and difficult to maintain. The relationship really still had *me* at the center. Everything was contingent upon *me* and my ability.

Finally, several years ago I was introduced to a "different" God, so to speak: One that loved me unconditionally and was pleased with me just because I am His child. This God did not need me to jump through any circus hoops to show Him how good I could be.

This God brought me rest and peace of mind as I was assured of my security in Him.

His love was not contingent upon my ability to perform. He loved me when I was doing well and loved me when I was in hell. He just loved me and there was no getting around it.

The relationship between me and my Creator changed dramatically since it was fueled not by authority (as we understand it) but by love. My new relationship with God invited me to boldly approach the throne of grace (*un*deserved favor).

This God hurt when I spoke negatively of myself or focused on my flaws.

This God encouraged what was good in me and spoke blessing over me.

This God did not expect me to perfect myself but, rather, offered to let me receive perfection. He considered me perfect.

This new relationship had *Him* at the center.

Once the dividing wall between myself and God came down and I began to embrace that I was already perfect in His eyes, my self-hatred began slipping away. The less I hated myself, the better my decision-making ability became. The more I felt loved, the more I loved. The more I love, the less likely I am to hurt myself or others.

Suddenly, I had a God that was not only doing "damage control" all the time, but a God who actually liked taking care of me. I was no longer a burden. Everything in my life became contingent upon *His* performance rather than my own. I simply surrendered to His will. The details were His to work out.

My surrender was not a disgruntled resolution but a gleeful hope and certain trust. It started as fearful and has gradually matured to the point where it is more fearful for me to try to manipulate my own life than it is to let Him have it.

This God is *much* easier to surrender completely to. This God is *for* me not against me. When I am struggling today, chances are good I have started trying to manage my life again. My recourse is not to try harder but rather to rest in Him. Return to my Source of peace, take a deep breath, and let Him take it from there. Reality is, He already has it; I am fighting Him for the wheel and wearing myself out.

How has Step 3 worked in your life?

I'm Jennifer. Thanks for letting me chair the meeting.

STEP 3 PRAYERS

from *The Big Book of Alcoholics Anonymous*, pp. 63, 59

God, I offer myself to Thee —
to build with me and to do with me
as Thou wilt.

Relieve me of the bondage of self,

that I may better do Thy will.

Take away my difficulties,

that victory over them

may bear witness to those I would help

of Thy Power,

Thy Love, and

Thy Way of life.

May I do Thy will always!

Amen.

*G*od, Take my will and my life. Guide me in my recovery.

Show me how to live. Amen.

STEP 4 MEETING
John Featherston, August 2014

Step 4: We made a searching and fearless moral inventory of
ourselves.

On page 58 of *The Big Book of Alcoholics Anonymous*, in the section
leading into the Steps, it says:

> If you have decided you want what we have and are willing to go
> to any length to get it—then you are ready to take certain steps.
> At some of these we balked….

For most of us, the first moment for "supreme balking" is Step 4! This
is where most of us stop our journey and miss the miracle. It says: "We
made a searching and fearless moral inventory of ourselves."

So, why would I want to sit down and put on paper the wrongs I have
done, and the wrongs done to me?

Almost all of the spiritual sicknesses that infect us and hurt us are
practiced in *secret* and in the *dark*. That is where our Enemy works. That
is how he wins. When we write them, when we inventory them, when
we speak them, they are dragged out into the light where the One who
is the Light can take them away and break the grip they have on us.

Okay, that's fine. But why do I have to write them down? Because then they become real. Truth has not always been one of our strongest attributes. The old saying in the circles I sit in says: "How can you tell when one of us is lying? Our lips are moving!!" Some of the best people I know sit in those circles. For good people to do bad things, consistently, we *have to lie*. The one we lie to most often is *ourself*.

For the hurts of our lives to come out of the dark places in our hearts—through a pen, and onto paper—makes them real. That is why the Big-BIG-Book says:

> Therefore confess your sins to each other and pray for each other so that you may be healed. The prayer of a righteous person is powerful and effective (James 5:16).

This is where that healing begins. This is the first piece of that healing process.

A few things to remember:

- We put to paper specifically how we have done harm to ourselves and others. The one we have hurt the most is ourself. Put those on paper, too.

- Step 4 does not say this is a "searching and fearless *immoral* inventory." The bad things need to see the light, but there is also real good in the worst of us. We also need a thorough inventory of the good in our life so we can feed and build on those good things. Write them down, too.

- *The Big Book* says that "resentment is the number one offender" in our staying spiritually sick. They fester in the dark; they will wither in the light, so we write down the hurts inflicted on us. Again, be specific.

So, for those of us who have worked this Step, what obstacles did you have to overcome to do this? What blessings came from it? What did you learn here?

For those who have not yet taken this Step, what is standing in your way? What are you afraid of? What do you hope to gain on the other side of it?

As always, this is your meeting. Please share your Step 4 experience, or whatever you need to talk about tonight.

Thanks for letting me chair the meeting on this step.

adapted from *The Big Book of Alcoholics Anonymous*, pg. 68

*G*od, relieve me of this fear
and direct my attention
to what You would have me be.
Amen.

Step 5 Meeting
Linda Widhalm, May 2014

Step 5: We admitted to God, to ourselves, and to another human being the exact nature of our wrongs.

The Devil and the Duck, A Story

Johnny and his sister, Sally, were visiting their grandparents on their farm one summer. Grandpa gave Johnny a slingshot, which he had whittled himself, to play with out in the woods. Johnny practiced all day but he could never hit the target. Frustrated, he headed back to the house for dinner.

As he was walking back he saw Grandma's pet duck. On an impulse, he took aim and let a rock fly from the slingshot. He hit the duck square in the head and killed it! He was shocked and grieved. In a panic, he hid the dead duck in the wood pile, only to see his sister watching!

Sally had seen it all, but she said nothing. After lunch the next day Grandma said, "Sally, let's wash the dishes." But Sally said, "Grandma, Johnny told me he wanted to help in the kitchen." Then she whispered to him, "Remember the duck?" Johnny did the dishes.

Later that day, Grandpa asked if the children wanted to go fishing and Grandma said, "I'm sorry, but I need Sally to help make supper." Sally just smiled and said, "Well, that's all right because Johnny told me he wanted to help." She whispered again, "Remember the duck?" Sally went fishing and Johnny stayed to help with dinner.

After several days of Johnny doing both his chores and Sally's, he finally couldn't stand it any longer. He came to Grandma and confessed that he had killed the duck. Grandma knelt down, gave him a hug, and said, "Sweetheart, I know. You see, I was standing at the window and I saw the whole thing. But because I love you,

I forgave you. I was just wondering how long you would let Sally make a slave of you."

Shame and guilt from past mistakes thrive in secrecy and darkness. That is what gives them power and makes you their slave. Guess what? God was "standing at the window and saw the whole thing"—along with everything on your Step 4 inventory. Like the grandmother in the story, He wants you to know that He loves you and that you are forgiven. He is just wondering how long you will let the devil make a slave of you.

God has a solution. James 5:16 (AMP) tell us to

> Confess to one another therefore your faults [your slips, your false steps, your offenses, your sins] and pray [also] for one another, that you may be healed and restored [to a spiritual tone of mind and heart]. The earnest [heartfelt, continued] prayer of a righteous man makes tremendous power available [dynamic in its working].

If you have taken a 5th Step, share with us what it was like. I'll go first.

I'm Linda. I'm an ...

Step 5 Prayer

from The Big Book of Alcoholics Anonymous, pg. 75

God, I thank You from the bottom of my heart
  that I know You better.
Help me become aware of anything
  I have omitted discussing with another person.
Help me to do what is necessary
  to walk a free man at last.
Amen.

STEP 6 MEETING
Kevin Kirkland, June 2013

Step 6: We were entirely ready to have God remove all these
defects of character.

A great counterbalance to most of our defects of character is compassion.
When we ask God to remove our defects of character, maybe we should
ask Him to replace it with compassion.

The principle of compassion lies at the heart of all religious, ethical,
and spiritual traditions. Compassion calls us to always treat others as
the golden rule says—as we would like to be treated ourselves.

Working tirelessly to alleviate the suffering of one another has the
desired affect of dethroning ourselves from the center of our world
and putting another there; to honor every single human being without
exception; to treat everyone with justice, fairness, and respect.

But Step 6 is not about us doing anything except getting ready to
let God do another of His works in our lives. I find it is a lot like the
progression of the first three Steps: admitting I'm powerless, He isn't,
and I'm going to let Him remove all my defects of character. But I also
know I will not submit to that if I do not see my defects of character are
what got me ensnared in the first place, then kept me there.

Those who have worked the Steps should be able to look back and see
defects of character God removed and recognized how your life has
changed as a result of God's work. Please share with us what it was
like, what happened, and what it is like now.

For me, personally, I lived in denial about my problems, about how
alcohol made them worse. I would not listen to anyone who tried
to help me. Denial was the first defect of character God needed to
remove for me to begin making progress. I had to stop denying so I
could become honest, but I could not stop denying on my own. I was
powerless over it.

When you are in denial, you do not attend meetings; you do not stay
sober; you do not have meaningful relationships with anyone, not even
your family.

Today I have meaningful relationships with family members whom
I had not seen in the many years I was living in denial. Now I attend
meetings and have many meaningful friendships here with you and
at Serenity Church. I still have problems, but I know who to turn to

with them: my Higher Power, Jesus Christ. And I do not deny them anymore.

I'm Kevin. Thanks for letting me chair the meeting.

Step 6 Prayer

from *The Big Book of Alcoholics Anonymous*, pg. 76

*G*od help me become willing to let go of all the things
   to which I still cling.
   Help me to be ready to let You remove all of these defects,
   that Your will and purpose may take their place.
   Amen.

Step 7 Meeting
Linda Widhalm, July 2014

Step 7: We humbly ask Him to remove our shortcomings.

Shortcomings are the defects of character which we were entirely ready to have God remove in Step 6.

A recovery buddy in my Step Study Class pulled me aside the other night to ask me about dealing with her defects of character. She said in doing the Step Study with us she had come to realize how judgmental she was. Over the course of a few weeks she had done her best to clamp her mouth shut when normally a judgmental remark would have come out. She said it was making her feel worse and worse about herself because the judgmental thoughts were not stopping.

I realized that she had been to the class on Step 6 but missed the class on Step 7. So I said, "The wonderful thing about Step 7 is that we don't have to get rid of our defects of character ourselves. That's God's job!"

All at once, tears filled her eyes, she gasped and her body jerked. "That's it! That's what I needed to know," she said.

I told her at the end of class we all got on our knees together and said the **Step 7 Prayer**:

My Creator, I am now willing that You should have all of me, good and bad. I pray that You now remove from me every single defect of character which stands in the way of my usefulness to You and my fellows. Grant me strength, as I go out from here, to do Your bidding. Amen (*The Big Book of AA*, pg. 76).

As she headed off to read that chapter and get on her knees, I marveled that it was only because I, too, was trying to get rid of my own character defects by willpower until that same lesson that I was able to see where she was hung up.

An indication for me that I am having character-defect issues is when I have some trouble that is mystifying me or that I want to blame on others.

Guess what? God is never mystified over what the problem is. It's me! So I return to my knees to lay down another defect of character that He has made evident to me. I did not mean to be hanging on to them, but I am finding my life is going better now that I consider this a maintenance step for me.

Maybe those defects of character were not standing in the way of my usefulness to Him and others before? I don't know. What I do know is that I do not have to let my defects of character twist a knot in me if I will hit my knees and ask Him to remove them.

Thanks for letting me chair the meeting tonight.

Step 8 Meeting
John Lanier, August 2014

Step 8: We made a list of all persons we had harmed and became willing to make amends to them all.

Do to others as you would have them do to you (Luke 6:31).

Up until this point in our recovery process our focus has been on ourselves—admitting our powerlessness (Step 1); acknowledging *His* power (Step 2); turning our will and lives over to the care of God (Step 3); doing our best to make an honest and thorough moral inventory of our lives (Step 4); admitting to ourselves, God, and another human being the exact nature of our wrongs (Step 5); becoming willing, then asking Him to remove those defects of character that stand in the way of our usefulness to God and our fellow human beings (Steps 6 and 7). Now we move towards developing "the best possible relations with every human being we know" (*Twelve Steps and Twelve Traditions*, pg. 77).

Step 8 is just a list and, yes, it is hard to focus on Step 8 without thinking ahead as we prepare to make amends in Step 9. But we must try to focus on the list only and to do it to the best of our ability.

By the time we have made a thorough list, have reviewed it with our sponsor and prayed for God to make us willing, we will be ready to make amends to those we have harmed and forgive those who have harmed us. *The Big Book* (Appendix II "Spiritual Experience," pg. 7) says,

> Willingness, honesty, and open-mindedness are the essentials of recovery. But these are indispensable.

Our Step 4 inventory will be helpful as we make our Step 8 list; however, there may be others that belong on the list. Working with our sponsor will help us here. By this Step, our sponsor has as good an understanding of us as anyone ever has before.

An example in my life of someone I added to my list are my kids; I did not resent them, so they were not on my Step 4 inventory, but I was not the father to them or the grandfather to their children that I know God intended me to be. That "harmed" them, so they went on the list. The reality of this filled me with guilt and shame for which I needed to forgive myself, so I went on the list, too.

The making of this list is not an easy task. *Twelve Steps and Twelve Traditions* says

> Whenever our pencil falters, we can fortify and cheer ourselves by remembering what [recovery] experience in this Step has meant to others. It is the beginning of the end of isolation from our fellows and from God (pg. 82).

So let's share some experience. What was it like when you were making your list?

Thank you for the privilege of letting me share my experience with Step 8.

Step 8 Prayer

adapted from *The Big Book of Alcoholics Anonymous*, pg. 76

*G*od help me to become willing to sweep away the debris of self-will and self-reliant living.
Thy will be done for this person as well as for me. Amen.

Step 9 Meeting
John Lanier, September 2014

Step 9: We made direct amends to such people wherever possible, except when to do so would injure them or others.

> Therefore, if you are offering a gift at the altar and there remember that your brother has something against you, leave your gift there in front of the altar. First go and be reconciled to your brother; then come and offer your gift (Matthew 5: 23-24).

For many of us, this Step seems overwhelming if not impossible. Remember, if we are diligent in working the previous eight Steps with a sponsor and maintaining the willingness the *Big Book* says is "indispensable," then we will be ready once we have completed Step 8.

Do not try to do this Step alone. The experience of a good sponsor is invaluable here. The value you will gain from a successful 9th Step amend will also be invaluable.

It is here during our journey, the *Big Book* says that

> If we are pains-taking about this phase of our development, we will be amazed before we are half way through (pp. 83-84).

Consider just the first promise, "we will know a new freedom and a new happiness." If we stopped there, wouldn't it be worth doing? Isn't it true that for most of our lives we have felt trapped in our sinful behavior, unable (or unwilling) to change our lives?

For me, I just wanted to be at peace and be "happy." Basically, that is why I drank, drugged, and lived the lifestyle I lived. As the prodigal son finally realized after he hit a true bottom, the Father loves us unconditionally no matter what we have done. That is how our Father loves us. And when He sees us afar off, He will run to us—not walk, but run—and kiss us, hug us, and bring us back home. Never to be alone again.

Step 9 is *for* us, not the person we have harmed. For us to remove the blockage that our past behavior has caused, we must do our level best at cleaning our side of the street.

It is not about how we are received when we make direct amends to those we harmed. We may be rejected all together. But we can be sure we will be free even if that is the case. The guilt and shame we have carried most of our lives for not addressing the harms we have done will fall away.

Once we have made amends, regardless of the outcome, we find freedom. Then we can move into forgiveness, even toward those who truly harmed us.

I would like to hear how your sponsor's insight has helped you with this Step, or what you hope to gain or did gain from making some amends.

Thank you for the privilege of sharing my experience with Step 9.

My name is John, and I am an overcomer.

STEP 9 MEETING ON AMENDS LISTS
John Lanier, September 2014

Step 9: We made direct amends to such people wherever possible, except when to do so would injure them or others.

> Restore to me the joy of Your salvation and grant me a willing spirit, to sustain me (Psalm 51:12).

It is suggested that we divide our amends into three lists:
   (a) those I am willing to make amends to now,
   (b) those who, with prayer and petition, I will become willing to make amends to sometime in the future, and
   (c) those I am convinced I will *never* make amends to.

Be careful with this concept, as we are the best in procrastination, self-righteousness, and denial. Work closely with your trusted sponsor and try not to delay this process. You will find as you make amends to the ones you put on the first list, "Willing to make amends to now," you will most likely see the second list move forward to where you become willing. And, yes, the No Nevers will most likely follow the same course.

Christ calls us to "love our enemies." He does not say we have to *like* them or have lifelong relationships with them. He calls us to "be reconciled to our brothers."

One of Webster's definitions of *reconcile* is to "resolve" a past wrong. That can be as simple, or as hard, as admitting you are wrong and being willing to "make things right" for whatever the wrong may have been.

Likewise, Webster defines *amend* as "to change or modify for the better." It is not always an apology; as a matter of fact, if we are not willing to change the behavior, we are not ready to make the amend.

I certainly experienced change in my willingness to make amends during the process of making my way through my list. How has it been for you?

Thank you for the privilege of sharing my experience with Step 9.

My name is John, and I am an overcomer.

STEP 9 PRAYER

from *The Big Book of Alcoholics Anonymous*, pp. 78-80

*G*od give me the strength and direction to do the right thing
   no matter what the consequences may be.
Help me to consider others and not harm them in any way.
Help me to consult with others before I take any actions
   that would cause me to be sorry.
Help me to not repeat such behaviors.
Show me the way of Patience, Tolerance, Kindliness, and Love
And help me live the spiritual life.
Amen.

STEP 10 MEETING
Lauri Lanier, August 2014

Step 10: We continued to take personal inventory and, when
   we were wrong, promptly admitted it.

Before I came into the program, my past haunted me often. I worried about running into certain people, felt ashamed of past behaviors, and did not have a clue how to fix any of it. The program has given me tools to clean up the past, as best I can, and keep today free from conflict, stress, and resentment.

I cleaned up my past—my side of the street—by doing Steps 4–9. Those Steps also taught me what I needed to know to continue to take personal inventory and promptly admit when I am wrong. I do not have to let things build up anymore; I can if I want to, but my "want to" has changed. I can no longer stand knowing I have screwed something up or harmed someone—things I used to drink and drug over. Today I have tools in the program that help me deal with life differently. One of those tools is Step 10.

The Big Book tells us we

> continue to watch for selfishness, dishonesty, resentment, and fear. When these crop up, we ask God at once to remove them. We discuss them with someone immediately and make amends quickly if we have harmed anyone. Then we resolutely turn our thoughts to someone we can help.

That is pretty simple! Not necessarily easy, but it is simple. Simple instructions that we can complicate the heck out of.

When I am upset, it is hard for me to think clearly about what has upset me. Now it has become a habit to pick up the phone and talk to someone in the program about what is happening that has me twisted. A sponsor can help us sort out whether we have been selfish, dishonest, resentful, or fearful. Then I need to, at once, ask God to remove the feelings that are disturbing me. A sponsor can also help me sort out if I have harmed anyone and if I need to make amends quickly.

I remember when I first started working Step 10 I told my sponsor I had lied about why I was late to work one day. It bothered me that I had lied! Go figure! My sponsor told me I needed to go to my boss, tell him I lied, then tell him the real reason I was late, which was that I had hit the snooze button too many times.

Having to tell him I had lied really stunk, but it kept me from lying in the future because I did not want to have to do that again! So, in this situation, I had been dishonest because I was fearful of being honest about why I was late. I asked God to remove the fear and then I had to go fix my dishonesty by telling the truth. Then, rather than worry about what might happen next, my sponsor told me to call someone else in the program and check on them. Get out of myself and turn my attention to someone else.

It is really that simple. Get help sorting out your feelings, ask God to remove what is causing your discomfort, make amends if necessary, and turn your attention to someone else. Put into daily practice what we learned in Steps 4 – 9. It works, if you work it!

Step 10 Prayer

from The Big Book of Alcoholics Anonymous, pg. 84

*G*od remove the selfishness, dishonesty, resentment, and fear that has cropped up in my life right now. Help me discuss this with someone immediately and make amends quickly if I have harmed anyone.

Help me to cease fighting anything and anyone, show me where I may be helpful to someone else.

Help me react sanely; not cocky or afraid.

How can I best serve You? Your will not mine be done.

Amen.

Step 11 Meeting
Michele Aboumrad, November 2014

Step 11: We sought through prayer and meditation to improve our conscious contact with God, as we understood Him, praying only for knowledge of His will for us and the power to carry that out.

My name's Michele. I'm an Overcomer.

I walked out on the patio on a relatively quiet night, settled into a chair, and a calm came over me, a readiness unlike ever before. At that moment I could almost feel my mind opening up as gently and gracefully as a white rose in the morning—glistening, unfolding life.

A bird sat on the gate column twitching around, but his eyeball was pointed at me as if God was saying, "My child, what are you doing? Can you hear Me? I know you hear and feel Me, just listen, breathe, and let Me process for you; for I am God, Jesus Christ, your Father—and I've got this."

So I sat and had a conversation with God, unrehearsed, unashamed, and with a spiritual feeling of no equal. No matter what, God cares. Aha—not an obnoxious aha, a really honest aha that left me with no doubt as to my journey.

While I feel it is important to read the Bible, I enjoy and understand so much from my meditation with God. So now I want to get into the word and read it with fresh eyes, open, and find a new unobstructed understanding within the stories and the Psalms and everything else.

Is my life perfect, why yes, it is. And I intend to make full progress at fitting myself into it. Even though I will only become perfect when I join God and His people in heaven, I can make my journey sour or I can "Let Go and Let God" and everything will be alright.

How has this step been for you?

STEP 11 MEETING ON MEDITATION
Linda Widhalm, November 2014

Step 11: We sought through prayer and meditation to improve our conscious contact with God, as we understood Him, praying only for knowledge of His will for us and the power to carry that out.

Some of us have gotten hung up on that word Meditation. It helped me when I realized mediation is not only one thing.

A daily e-mail devotional I subscribed to describes meditation like this:

> *Meditate* means to murmur, imagine, study, talk, or make plans in the mind. It means to roll a thought over and over in the mind until it becomes smooth and acceptable. When we consider a promise of God, it is important to process that thought by rolling it over in our spirit until it begins to speak to us.

> Light and revelation will come into our spirits, causing life and fruitfulness. God's Word will then take hold of our imaginations and begin to transform our thoughts. We will begin to imagine change and then start making plans in our minds to bring about those changes. And because we are conforming to God's Word and His Will, He causes us to prosper.

This describes the process that happens when we "change our stinkin' thinkin'." It does not happen all at once. We allow new information in rather than rejecting it right away. We ask God to help us. Then we mull it over. We may use our imagination to view some of our life circumstances differently in the light of this new information. Before we know it, we are seeing things differently. Negative thoughts no longer have a home.

When I first came into recovery I kept hearing Trina make statements about how her husband's actions were none of her business. I had absolutely *no understanding* of that statement. It went against everything I was raised to understand about being a wife and mother. As much as I mulled it over on my own, I got *nothing*! Then I asked God to help me understand. He began showing me the boundary lines between what was my stuff and what was not.

Yes, what other people do and say affects me; but it is not my responsibility to "head them off at the pass," to keep them from making what I think is a mistake.

I do not need to give them my advice unless they ask me for it. It is not my business if they take my advice or leave it. This understanding freed me from trying to predict the future about what my husband, children, or others might *need*, and from having to provide for that need before they asked.

The Serenity Prayer applied to life situations helps with that a lot, too. Romans 8:6 says,

> The mind governed by the flesh is death, but the mind governed by the Spirit is life and peace.

Step 11 is a lot about changing Who is governing our minds.

STEP 11 PRAYER

adapted from *The Big Book of Alcoholics Anonymous*, pp. 87-88

*G*od, I'm agitated and doubtful right now.
  Help me to stop and remember that I've made a decision
    to let You be my God.
  Give me the right thoughts and actions.
  God save me from fear, anger, worry, self-pity,
    or foolish decisions, that Your will not mine be done.
  Amen.

Step 12 Meeting I
Pat Widhalm, December 2014

Step 12: Having had a spiritual awakening as the result of
these Steps, we tried to carry this message to others
and to practice these principles in all our affairs.

Hi, I'm Pat. I'd like to read the prayer by St. Francis of Assisi:

*L*ord, make me a channel of thy peace,
    that where there is hatred, I may bring love;
that where there is wrong, I may bring the spirit of forgiveness;
that where there is discord, I may bring harmony;
that where there is error, I may bring truth;
that where there is doubt, I may bring faith;
that where there is despair, I may bring hope;
that where there are shadows, I may bring light;
that where there is sadness, I may bring joy.

Lord, grant that I may seek rather to comfort
    than to be comforted;
to understand, than to be understood;
to love, than to be loved.

For it is by self-forgetting that one finds.
It is by forgiving that one is forgiven.
It is by dying that one awakens to Eternal Life.

When we first started working the Steps, it was tough. Maybe you did
not know how you would make it to the next minute, let alone "One
day at a time." But you wanted to make it, so you did whatever your
sponsor told you whether it made sense to you or not, no matter how
difficult it seemed.

Yet, at first it didn't seem to make any difference, so you would just
"fake it to make it," always doing the "next right thing." As time
passed and you kept working the Steps, perhaps without realizing it,
the promises started to materialize and things seemed to get a little
easier. Then one day you "suddenly realized that God was doing for
you what you could not do for yourself." And not only that, you "had
lost interest in selfish things and gained interest in others"; you had a
"spiritual awakening" because God was using you as a "channel of His
peace," and you were finding your own peace by lifting someone else
out of the pit.

Tonight I would like us to talk about your most memorable experience with "suddenly realizing," and to hear how you carried this message to others.

Thanks for letting me chair the meeting.

Step 12 Meeting II
Jennifer (Horton) Michie, December 2011

Step 12: Having had a spiritual awakening as a result of these steps, we tried to carry this message to others, and to practice these principles in all our affairs.

Key points:

1. **We had a spiritual awakening**   Spiritual awakening is the predecessor for carrying the message and the successful practice of the principles of recovery. The awakening of our hearts to Love—which is God—is what allows us to "carry," literally "like a pregnancy," our message and to appropriate the principles in all aspects of our lives.

2. **We carry the message**   Again, this carrying strikes me more as a carrying from the inside like a woman carries a child within her. The best way for others to see and understand what our lives represent is for that message to become larger and larger and, essentially, "bigger" or more visible to others even without words.

3. **We practice these principles in *all* our affairs**   The principles of love and forgiveness, which are the basic nutshell of the program, should naturally permeate every area of our life as we mature in this recovery walk. It begins with getting our addiction out of the way so we can appropriate this into other areas of our life including our relationships and our general response to the world around us.

Carrying the message involves three major concepts: Let, Listen, and Give. If we truly desire to give hope to others, we must understand these.

1. **Listen**   We cannot help anyone unless we are able to hear them. If people do not feel heard, they will not care about what we may have to offer. By listening, our own hearts become humble and we may gain someone else's permission to speak into a painful area of their life. Listening shows them we care about them and see them as a

person apart from the destructive behaviors that are harming them and others.

2. **LET** To "let" is essentially to "not hinder." Some examples of "let" in the *Big Book* include:

> Let him draw his own conclusion, let him talk, let him ask, let him choose his own concept of God, let him see, and let him follow his own conscience.

It is important that we do not hinder this process.

3. **GIVE**: Give him space, give him time, give him support, give him your ear, and give him your help.

Remember that the "fix it" mentality fails to save addicts and usually increases their frustration. *The Big Book* tells us not to "moralize or lecture" and not to pressure (pg. 91). We have stopped fighting anybody or anything we are carrying.

I'm Jennifer. Thanks for letting me chair the meeting.

DAILY PRAYERS

from The Big Book of Alcoholics Anonymous, pg. 86

MORNING

> God direct my thinking today so that it be divorced of self-pity, dishonesty, self-will, self-seeking, and fear. God inspire my thinking, decisions, and intuitions. Help me to relax and take it easy. Free me from doubt and indecision. Guide me through this day and show me my next step. God give me what I need to take care of any problems. I ask all these things that I may be of maximum service to you and my fellow man. Amen.

NIGHT

> God forgive me where I have been resentful, selfish, dishonest, or afraid today. Help me to not keep anything to myself but to discuss it all openly with another person; show me where I owe an apology and help me make it. Help me to be kind and loving to all people. Use me in the mainstream of life, God. Remove worry, remorse, or morbid reflections that I may be of usefulness to others. Amen.

On a Coin or Slogan

Coin: Butterfly
The Story of the Butterfly
(Author unknown)
Kim Mladjen, September 2006

Hi. I'm Kim, and I'm a grateful Overcomer.

A man found a cocoon of a butterfly. One day a small opening appeared. He sat and watched the butterfly for several hours as it struggled to squeeze its body through the tiny hole. Then it stopped, as if it could not go further. So the man decided to help the butterfly.

He took a pair of scissors and made the hole larger. The butterfly emerged easily but it had a swollen body and shriveled wings. The man continued to watch it, expecting any minute the wings would enlarge and expand enough to support the body; but that is not what happened. In fact, the butterfly spent the rest of its life crawling around. It was never able to fly.

What the man in his kindness and haste did not understand was that the restricting cocoon and the struggle required by the butterfly to get through the opening is the way fluid is forced from the body into the wings preparing them for flight.

Struggles are exactly what we need in our lives, too. Going through life with no obstacles would cripple us. We need struggles to make us stronger. So, too, others need to do their own struggling. It may seem merciful, but saving them from it cripples them.

We would like to hear your experience, strength, and hope about the benefits you have seen come from the obstacles you have struggled through.

Thanks for letting me chair tonight.

Coin: The Starfish
Linda Widhalm, August 2008

Hello, I'm Linda. I'm an Overcomer. I have something for each of you tonight. [Pass out the starfish coin and/or a starfish purchased at a hobby store.]

Starfish on a beach are a daytime reminder of the promise God made to Abraham in Genesis 22:17:

> I will surely bless you and make your descendants as numerous as the stars in the sky and the sand on the seashore.

Stars and sand in the same verse in Scripture. You are a descendant of Abraham by blood. Maybe, like my dad, and me, you can say which tribe you likely descended from. Even better, the blood of Jesus has made you a blood descendant. You matter.

You are the continuing fulfillment of Jesus' promise in John 14:20:

> On that day you will realize that I am in My Father, and you are in Me and I am in you.

Starfish become stranded on the beach when the tide goes out because they need water to move. They push and pull water through tubes in their rays which causes them to move.

What Jesus said in John 14:20 always confused me a bit. Contemplating the starfish helped me understand the truth of this verse. If "you" are the starfish, and Jesus is the seawater, and the Father is the ocean, then when the starfish is in the ocean, the seawater is also in the starfish. "On that day you will realize that I/seawater am in My Father/ocean, and you/starfish are in Me/seawater and I/seawater am in you/starfish" (John 14:20 adapted).

This also brings new understanding to the verse in Acts where Paul is talking to the "Men of Athens" and says,

> 'For in Him we live and move and have our being.' As some of your poets have said, 'We are his offspring' (Acts 17:28).

Without Him, we become stranded, exposed, and dry up.

When I gave you the starfish many of you acted like I was giving you a treasure. How much more of a treasure is a living starfish, gracefully moving in the habitat God created for it to live in.

I know I've had times of being dried up, unable to function, but let's focus on how all that dryness has been overcome with Jesus moving through us and giving us the power to move.

Thanks for letting me chair the meeting

COIN: POWERLESS, BUT NOT HELPLESS
(Things Do Not Change, We Do)
Pat Widhalm, June 2009

I was born in 1951. Back then kids did not command the same rights and respect as adults. We were expected to do as we were told and to not ask questions, regardless of who the adult might be.

Perhaps that is why, when I was five years old and needed to have my tonsils removed, no one felt it necessary to explain to me what was about to happen. I was passed off to a couple of nurses who dressed me in a hospital gown and put me on a wheeled table then rolled me into a brightly lit room with all kinds of stainless steel equipment and giants with covered faces—I knew they were doctors.

I was very apprehensive, but one nurse was very kind to me and tried to comfort me by reading a story about a mother donkey and her baby; it settled me down—until they wanted to administer anesthesia.

I know now they were using ether, but at the time I had no idea what they planned to do and I became frightened again. They put a cloth across my nose and mouth and, at the first drip of the strange smelling substance, I panicked and tried to bolt from the table, causing quite a disturbance. One of the giants became quite angry with me and forcibly placed me back on the table. He had someone tie down my arms and legs while someone else held my head still, all the while I am screaming at the top of my lungs in absolute terror! When they put the cloth back across my nose and mouth and started dripping the ether again, I was convinced I was about to die and I went beyond terror, losing control of everything and making quite a mess of myself. The last thing I remember is the wet, clinging hospital gown and the shame I felt as the angry giant derided me for being such a bad boy.

To this day I remember that event with vivid detail, and I have this irrational fear of doctors, medical procedures of any kind, and especially hospital gowns. When it comes to doctors and medical procedures, I can reason my way through my feelings, but hospital gowns are a different matter. Whenever I try to wear a hospital gown, it is like I am back on that table; the same feelings of terror and shame well up inside me and my only way of dealing with them is to retreat into this little place in my head, try to hold them at bay.

Because I was so ashamed of what I was feeling, I never told anyone what I was going through for over 50 years. That is a long time to be powerless and a long time to keep a secret.

When I was a much younger man it was not hard to keep my secret— I hardly ever went to a doctor and never had much need to wear a hospital gown. But dark secrets have a way of catching up to you. After I got married I would resist my wife's urging to see a doctor unless I was on death's doorstep. I managed to get by that way until I was diagnosed with cancer in my leg in 1989—a diagnosis that required an operation, a three-day stay in the hospital, and several weeks of radiation treatments, all requiring a hospital gown. It was a horrible experience. I kept my secret—but at a price. While holding my fears at bay, my wife felt as if I was pushing her away as well, and it hurt my relationship with her. But, still, I kept my secret.

In 2009, something unexpected happened. I was having recurring sinus infections and needed a small day operation to clean out my sinuses. I had been prepped for the surgery and was dutifully wearing the hospital gown provided—holding my fears at bay until we received word the doctor had a minor emergency to attend to and would be unavoidably delayed. You would think after dealing with this fear for so long it would get easier, but it does not. If anything, it becomes harder each time.

Now, with this unexpected disruption in routine, I was losing my concentration. I felt the panic coming on and there was nothing I could do. Somehow my wife picked up on my feelings and asked me what was going on. I broke down and confessed my fear to both her and the nurse attending me, expecting to be laughed at over such a silly thing. But they did not laugh; they only asked how they could help me.

I was amazed. I could not think of anything to help except maybe singing, remembering the nurse who had read to me. To my surprise my nurse sang me a lullaby and then she came back with two more nurses and they all sang to me. The singing did help for a bit, but still the doctor had not come and panic was rising once again. It was then my wife suggested a simple solution: remove the gown!

I had never considered the possibility before. It was such a simple answer, and it worked. I cannot say all my fear vanished, but the panic subsided and I made it through the operation.

After that experience I went to see my family doctor and told him the whole story. He was able to convince me what had happened to me as a child was not my fault and I did not have to be ashamed of what I had felt for so many years.

People will help you if you tell them what you need. My doctor gave me a letter of explanation that I can play as my "get out of jail free card" whenever there is a procedure requiring a hospital gown. But I have found that I seldom have to play it. I tell my nurse or doctor what I need. The hospital gown is there for peoples' comfort and dignity and, although a little unusual, my comfort and dignity happens to have a different need. I have never worn another hospital gown since that fateful day.

Yes, I am powerless over my feelings; but I have discovered I am not helpless. If I am honest about what I need, there will be someone who can help me.

Share on this topic or whatever is on your mind.

Thanks for letting me chair the meeting.

COIN: BUTTERFLY / SLOGAN: LET GO AND LET GOD
Trina Hightower

I'm Trina, and I'm an overcomer!!

At Overcomers, we hand out monthly coins with recovery slogans on one side and a picture on the opposite side. My favorite is the Butterfly/ Let Go and Let God coin.

Butterflies are beautiful insects, but they do not start their lives as beautiful butterflies. They start as caterpillars that move very slowly, crawling through the dirt and on trees. To become a butterfly, the caterpillar metamorphoses or goes through extreme change. If during metamorphosis they are disturbed, they come out injured or deformed and not as God intended.

In my disease, I tried to force the change I wanted in my husband. I was physically, verbally, and emotionally abusive. In recovery, I learned that it was none of my business to change someone else's life, only to change my own. I learned if I trusted God, let go of those things that were not mine, and gave them over to God, He would take care of them with His Almighty power.

I have learned through trusting Him that the picture I have of how things should look is so microscopic and bland compared to His majestic masterpiece. I know now to Let Go and Let God!

Thanks for letting me chair the meeting. I'm Trina.

Slogan: One Day at a Time
Lael Barker, August 2014

My name's Lael, and I'm an Overcomer.

Of course one slogan we always hear as we come into recovery is "One Day at a Time." I had been in the rooms of AA for six months before I was ready to surrender and quit drinking. I never understood why they said just "one day at a time."

So there I was, sitting on my patio, maybe two weeks sober, and still "white knuckling it." I was wondering how I was ever going to make it without a drink for the rest of my life. I remember my mind going high speed into thoughts such as, "what about parties, what about graduations, what about my wedding (should that ever happen)— WAIT! FOREVER?!? What was I thinking?!"

I proceeded to accelerate into a near panic attack. It was then the Holy Spirit told me, "No, just for today. All you have to worry about is today."

My anxiety immediately eased and my breathing returned to normal. I thought to myself, "Ohhhh! *That's* why they say one day at a time!" I finally understood why I only have to worry about not drinking for today. Yes, there were times I had to break it down to hours or minutes at a time, but the Lord held true to His promise that He would help me on my walk through recovery, just as He said He would on the day I surrendered.

Jesus said in Matthew 6:33-34,

> But seek first His kingdom and His righteousness, and all these things will be added to you. So do not worry about tomorrow; for tomorrow will care for itself. Each day has enough trouble of its own.

I would like to hear how this or any other slogan has helped you through a tough moment.

I'm Lael. I'm an Overcomer. Thanks for letting me chair the meeting.

Coin: Let Go and Let God
Jennifer (Horton) Michie, 2009

I'm Jennifer. I'm an Overcomer.

I think what makes this a hard thing to do is we have identified ourselves so closely with the thing (whatever it may be) that we are trying to let go of. Whatever we are holding onto has become part of us, and in order to let it go we must face our fears of what will become of us when it is gone.

Several years ago a friend told me he was afraid to quit drinking because he did not know who he was sober. This fear encompasses much more than the obvious addictions. What will become of me if I let go of—

— drinking/drugs? Who am I when I'm sober? How will I handle difficult life situations if I cannot "escape" them?

What will become of me if I let go of—

— control? How can I feel strong without this [illusion of] control?

— fear? What guarantees do I have in life if I walk through this fear?

— sadness? If I let go of grief or sadness does it mean I do not remember? Will I still feel alive? Will the one I am grieving still know I love them?

— anger? If I'm no longer angry, where does that leave my heart? Will I be more vulnerable? Will I get hurt again?

— this unhealthy relationship? Does that mean I have failed? Will I find love again?

For years I struggled with serious control issues with my drug-addicted spouse. I felt his behavior was somehow my responsibility to correct. His behavior, in my mind, was a direct reflection on me as a person. It represented my success or my failure. I was obsessed with trying to fix him. I bore the weight of his poor choices. When he messed up, I covered up or cleaned up the mess. When I was afraid he would mess up, I nagged incessantly. I thought I was helping him but really I was protecting myself. I did not want to feel the guilt, failure, and so forth that was actually *his* to feel. I was feeling it all for him thus allowing him to hide behind me and not have to feel anything or take any responsibility because he had me to sort it all out.

One day as I was observing my five-year-old daughter and baby son interacting, I had an epiphany. Every time the baby started to do something he was not supposed to do, in spite of my presence, my daughter rushed to deal with him. I yelled, "I am right here!" I, as his *mother*, chose not to rush to him so I could see how far he would take the action before I dealt with it. "Every time I try to deal with him," I told her, "I have to get around *you* first! Please stop!"

Suddenly, I saw myself and my husband. I realized that if I wanted God to work things out in my husband, I was going to have to get out of the way.

I laid on the floor in the other room, face down, sobbing in the carpet, and released it all to God. It was hard and painful but the payoff has been very rewarding.

Fear of the unknown is very scary. It is hard to let "all things become new." I would like to hear your stories of times that you took the leap of faith, how you let go of something you feared to let go of, and what happened when you did.

I'm Jennifer. Thanks for letting me chair.

Slogan: Live and Let Live
Renée Bagbey, August 2014

My name is Renée. I'm an Overcomer.

If I were to pick a slogan that has been the most meaningful to me for the past 30 days, I would definitely have to say, "Live and Let Live." This slogan tells me the most about loving others just as they are and where they are in this thing we call Life.

In God's eyes, we are all level at the foot of the cross. When we cannot see each other through the lens of God's perfect Love, this slogan reminds me that God's Love heals, protects, and embraces. It simply never fails.

Share on this slogan, or any other recovery slogan that has helped you.

Thanks for letting me chair the meeting.

Additional Shares On Favorite Slogans:

- I'm Uncle Bill. My favorite? That's easy. "Don't quit before the miracle happens." I kept quitting before it happened, until this time!

- I'm Brennon. I'm an Overcomer. When I am in my head, I am behind enemy lines.

- I'm Jim W. Isolation is the darkroom where I develop my negatives.

- Mac Martin. My problem is Mac and alcohol makes is worse. ... After 7 years it has gotten easier, but it still takes the whole *#%! day.

- Mac Martin. I already knew these slogans to be true, I just had not accepted them as being fact. They helped me to realize that the 12 Step Program was actually a simple program. It was just hard.

But by the program being simple it gave me hope that I could do it. I heard someone in the program say they have never heard of anyone being too dumb to get the program, but there are a lot of intellectuals out there living under bridges.

This is my favorite saying that helped me: There is no problem so bad that a drink won't make worse. A drink won't change what just happened. It is just going to change what's fixin' to happen.

- *Macisms*: We attribute these to Mac Martin even though he may have heard them elsewhere. He sure knows how to use them at the right time, so we give him credit:

  I knew I could quit on my own, I'd done it a hundred times before!

  That's why they call it alcoho*li*sm and not alcohol*was*m.

  We would rather feel bad about the damage done than get an estimate for the cost of repairs.

  —instead of picking up that 500 pound phone and calling someone.

  When I came into AA they told me I would go a long way in AA because I had a long way to go!

On a Reading or Promise

Why I Needed a Sponsor
and to Begin Working the Steps Right Away
Che' Hightower

My name's Che', and I'm an Overcomer.

The Big Book of Alcoholics Anonymous says on page 24:

> The fact is that most alcoholics, for reasons yet obscure, have lost the power of choice in drink. Our so-called will power becomes practically nonexistent. We are unable, at certain times, to bring into our consciousness with sufficient force the memory of the suffering and humiliation of even a week or a month ago. We are without defense against the first drink.

You can substitute whatever your addiction or weakness is for the word "alcoholics" and "drink." It still applies. If you cannot seem to hold on to your sober mind for long, it is probably because you have not accepted the wisdom of these words, and gotten a sponsor, *and* started *working* the steps. As Mike Rosser says (with an Aussie accent):

> The goal here isn't a pocket full of red coins! A pocketful of red coins is not evidence of a desire; doing whatever is necessary so there is no relapse *is*. There's no such thing as a slip!

> Doing what hurts us is evidence of *not* doing the things we know we should do.

Attending meetings can serve as your memory because you will identify yourself in the stories other people share. You cannot trust your own memory to keep you sober. If you want to get better, you need a sponsor. You need to work the steps. You need to attend meetings. You need to listen to what your recovery buddies share. You need to share your own stories to keep them at the forefront of your mind. You have something to share yourself at every meeting not just to help the newcomer, but to remind yourself.

When I came out of treatment, I was determined to do whatever people who had recovered told me to do so I would make it. They told me to do 90 meetings in 90 days, so I did twice that! I got a sponsor. I started working the steps. My sponsor told me to share at every meeting, so I did. I tried to be as honest as I could be. I listened and I shared.

Share on what you did to hold onto your recovery. Or if you are struggling to hold onto it, now is a good time to share with us what you think you are missing, and let us help you get started on a road that will lead to recovery.

My name's Che'. Thanks for letting me chair the meeting.

ACCEPTANCE AND EXPECTATIONS
John Featherston

adapted from "Doctor, Addict, Alcoholic" by Dr. Paul O.
in *The Big Book of Alcoholics Anonymous*, pg. 418

I'm John. I'm an Overcomer.

My first sponsor noticed that most of our encounters with one another included me saying, "If he would just..." or, "If she would just..." or, "If they would just — then...." He gave me an assignment to read this reading from the *Big Book* every morning, and again every night, and any time I lost my serenity during the day:

> Acceptance is the answer to all my problems today. When I am disturbed, it is because I find some person, place, thing, or situation—some fact of my life—unacceptable to me, and I can find no serenity until I accept that person, place, thing, or situation as being exactly the way it is at this moment.

> I need to concentrate not so much on what needs to be changed in the world as on what needs to be changed in me and in my attitudes. Acceptance has taught me that there is a bit of good in the worst of us and a bit of bad in the best of us; that we each have a right to be here. When I focus on what's good today, I have a good day, and when I focus on what's bad, I have a bad day. If I focus on a problem, the problem increases; if I focus on the answer, the answer increases.

> When I focus on people's bad qualities, they multiply; when I focus on people's good qualities, they seem to grow and grow.

> Perhaps the best thing of all for me is to remember that my serenity is inversely proportional to my expectations. The higher my expectations of other people are, the lower is my serenity. I can watch my serenity level rise when I discard my expectations. I have to discard my 'rights' as well as my expectations by asking myself, "How important is it, really? How important is it compared to my serenity, my emotional sobriety?"

I do whatever is in front of me to be done, and let go of the results. I must keep my magic magnifying mind on my level of acceptance. When I remember this, I can see I've never had it so good.

To this day, I carry a laminated copy of the first paragraph in my wallet to remind myself, as often as needed.

I'm John. Thanks for letting me chair.

PROMISE 2 MEETING
Linda Widhalm, May 2015

Promise 2: We will not regret the past nor wish to shut the
        door on it.

Good evening, Everybody. I'm Linda, and I'm an Overcomer.

When I first heard this promise I thought it was crazy and ridiculous. Over time, while working the Steps and listening to others share their stories honestly, I realized that for me, my response to this promise was mainly due to shame.

I had been sick a lot as a kid. Sickness may not be the fault of anyone, but it still inconveniences a lot of people. Besides affecting me, my family had to cancel outings and parties, re-appropriate the family money, as well as devote time and energy to making childcare arrangements, doctors' appointments, and the like. No one ever intentionally blamed me for this but I still felt it was my fault. It is hard to miss realizing when your family is disappointed.

Since this described the first eight years of my life, I became a shame and blame magnet. It did not seem to matter whose fault something was, I felt the shame and took the blame. It does not make sense, I know, but that is how I lived a lot of my life.

Once I realized this, with the help of a sponsor, I began practicing *not* taking the blame for situations happening around me. I wish I could describe it for you, but it was very freeing for me. This helped me be able to know and deal with my own true issues. Another result was that I stopped resenting others for how I felt, or became less likely to do so.

You may think this strange magnetism does not describe you at all. It may not. Two common identifiers are: a parent who feels ashamed when their child does something wrong, or a family member of an addict who keeps the big secret of everything that goes on behind closed doors because they feel ashamed.

The truth is, it was hard for me to not want to shut the door on the parts of my past that were not really about me. Those parts are "not my business," as Trina would say. Everything else now constitutes my experience, strength, and hope!

I'm Linda. I hope I did not confuse you too much! Share on anything you want to about this promise.

SHARE: I'm Cyndy. I am an Overcomer.

I think that your introduction makes perfect sense, especially coming from an Al Anon or Codependents Anonymous point of view. This is good because sometimes people from this perspective may not relate to those things shared by the addict or alcoholic point of view.

I totally get it because I spent my first five years of sobriety very active in CODA and dealing with the effects of others blaming me without acknowledging their part in it. This caused a lot of resentment, and I wanted to just shut the door on all of it.

I had such a love/hate relationship with my parents, particularly, and I wanted to just move on, sober, and not deal with the causes and concerns behind it. From the alcoholic side of it, I wanted to shut the door on it because of the terrible guilt I felt over what I put my parents through, not to mention the shame I felt about the things I had done.

My problem was that I was so defensive about my part in it I got stuck in blaming others so I could totally bypass dealing with the guilt of my own behavior. So, what I think we are really talking about are two sides of the same coin. Hence, the phrase, "we are as sick as our secrets."

Regardless of what perspective you bring to the table, it is all about relationships (with ourselves, others, and most importantly, Jesus). Shame, blame, guilt, and denial are all pieces of the same puzzle. If we shut the door on it, we cannot learn how to love ourselves, and probably do not have a desire to help others by sharing our experience, strength, and hope with them.

Thanks for letting me share.

Promises 3 and 4 Meeting
Anonymous

Promise 3: We will comprehend the word *serenity*—

Promise 4: —and we will know peace.

Hello, Everyone.

I used to think that a peaceful life must mean a boring life. I could not even comprehend life without continual problems and crises. If there was not some drama going on in my life, I was likely to create one so I did not have to deal with what was going on inside of or around me. Obviously an emergency takes priority over the mess in my head, the unpaid bills, the messy house, the uncut grass, and relationship issues. Other people probably described me as a drama queen.

Seeking a peaceful, serene life is not what drove me into recovery. Not wanting to die, basically, from my own hand putting mind-numbing food into my mouth is what drove me here. If there was no drama to focus my attention away from thinking about my inner problems, food worked just as well.

Since working the steps with a sponsor, maintaining abstinence, and attending meetings regularly, I have discovered a whole new life I never thought possible. I have found that a peaceful life is *not* boring at all! I actually enjoy dealing with the things I used to avoid because now I have the proper tools to help me. And I do not have to do it alone. If I hit a snag, I do not have to retreat into old habits; I keep moving forward by picking up the phone or going to a meeting.

Accepting myself as I am has been huge for me. That is what has brought the most inner peace. I can now accept myself with my imperfections knowing they do not spoil all that is good within me. Like the saying, "Don't throw the baby out with the bath water," I find I am able to quietly reflect on my inner self, with love for myself, seeking the shortcoming that has muddied the water and needs to be worked on rather than avoided.

Now that I am more serene on the inside, there is more peace on the outside!

This meeting is for you. Be sure you get what you came for by sharing.

Thanks for letting me chair the meeting.

Promise 9 Meeting
Cyndy Sanders, May 2015

Promise 9: Our whole attitude and outlook upon life will change.

Hi, Everybody. I'm Cyndy, and I'm a very grateful Overcomer.

It is amazing how the process of working the Steps affects your perception of life. It changed my attitude because I finally realized, at a gut level, it truly is not all about me. As mentioned in *The Big Book of Alcoholics Anonymous* on pg. 84: "Love and tolerance of others is our code." I stopped looking at everything in terms of what is in it for me. My outlook was more concerned with what can I do for the other person.

It seemed if I could just keep my focus on Jesus Christ, the way I saw others was no longer judgmental or condemning. As Paul indicates in Ephesians, by having the eyes of your heart flooded with the Light, you can know and understand the hope to which He has called you. This is what I love about Serenity and our sharing in Overcomers. Because we clearly identify Jesus Christ as our Higher Power, as we work our way through the Steps, we actually begin to see things through His eyes. Please share on how your whole attitude and outlook upon life has changed.

I'm Cyndy. Thanks for letting me chair the meeting.

Promise 12 Meeting
or Cleaning Up the Mess
Lisa Watson, September 2014

Promise 12: We will suddenly realize that God is doing for us what we could not do for ourselves.

I'm Lisa. I'm an Overcomer.

Raise your hand if you were born. Now raise your hand if, when you were born, your hair was perfectly combed and you had fresh clean clothes on. That's ridiculous! Not a single baby has been born that way!

Babies are born covered in amniotic fluid, cheesy vernix, blood, and if we are honest, a fair number are born covered in poop. We do not expect newborns to clean themselves up before they emerge. We expect that cleaning up the mess will be one of the very first things we do for them. We do it because we love them.

God does not expect us to join His family with our mess already taken care of. He expects to do that for us. Because He loves us more than anything.

There have been many times that my baby has cried for me and I have found her with a leaky diaper. Or she's gotten sick and it is all over her and her crib. It would be ridiculous of me to expect her to clean that up on her own! All I expect is for her to cry while I clean it up for her. I will do it because I love her.

God knows there will be messes so big we are powerless to even help with the cleanup. He expects to handle those on His own. He will comfort us while we cry through the uncomfortable process because He loves us more than anything!

The other day a glass fell and shattered on the floor while Merry was emptying the dishwasher. She was up on the counter with bare feet. Merry is very capable and has cleaned up a *lot* of messes in her eight short years, but this time I tip-toed through the glass, put her on my back, and carried her a safe distance away. I knew she was not ready for this kind of mess. I cleaned it up for her and cut my own hand in the process.

God knows that even the most capable of us will face messes we are not prepared to handle. He is willing to shed His own blood while He cleans it up for us. Because He loves us more than anything!

A couple of months ago my husband came to Serenity Church but returned home because he was not feeling well. He left our five kids here with me but drove home in the van. Later he was having chest pains and needed to go to the ER, so I went to my mother and told her what was going on—that I needed to go check on my husband but had no way to get the kids home. She did not say, "Lisa, you are 28 years old! I already taught you how to drive a car and how to take care of children! Why are you bothering me with this?" She knew my knowledge and experience were not enough, so she drove my kids home and took care of them for me.

God knows that the oldest and most experienced of us will find ourselves in situations where our age, our wisdom, our life experiences are not enough. He wants us to remember that no matter how old we are, we are His precious children and He is always telling us, "I love you more than anything. I love you more than anything. I love *you* more than *any*thing! Look what I did for you!"

What is your experience with this promise?

Thanks for letting me chair the meeting.

Promise 12 Meeting
Cyndy Sanders, May 2015

Promise 12: We will suddenly realize that God is doing for us what we could not do for ourselves.

Hi, Everybody. I'm Cyndy, and I'm a very grateful Overcomer.

Perhaps one of the greatest epiphanies when working the Steps is the realization that God is doing for us what we cannot do for ourselves. In order to fully embrace the Steps we must completely surrender all to God. The promises are not only from the fruits of our efforts, but also a gift through the grace and mercy of the Lord.

Proverbs 3:5 tells us to lean on God and not on our own understanding. Initially, that sounded simple enough to me. I thought I had fully accepted this when I did Step 3. And I did, to some extent, but I guess it is human nature to want to take that control back.

In the *Big Book* it says as we begin Step 10 we have entered the world of the Spirit, and in order to remain spiritually fit we must not let up on our spiritual program of action. The beautiful thing about this is the way God changes us from the inside out. I want to pray for God to use me to help others, thirst to know more from the Word, and long to lead a more Christ-like life. Philippians 4:13 states in the Amplified Version that

> I have strength for all things in Christ Who empowers me [I am ready for anything ... through Him Who infuses inner strength into me].

Through the Steps, I began to let go of pride and other character defects. Once I realized I was a humble servant, God was able to use me as a vessel to do His work.

This can be exemplified by comparing my Saturdays before and after I worked the Steps. Before, I focused on what party I was going to that night, what was I going to wear, and whether I needed to go shopping.

However, once I began to accept my total reliance on God, my focus on what was important in life changed. A typical Saturday now consists of a trip to Serenity Church Metro in South Dallas in the morning to serve the homeless, the Serenity Church service that night, and an Overcomers meeting scheduled afterwards.

Once I realized I needed the Holy Spirit to work through me to help others, the change on the inside had started. For example, as we build relationships with the people in South Dallas, I find I am as blessed, if not more, than those I am there to serve.

When I came to God broken, seeking a solution for my earthly problems, He answered with a love that spiritually would change my whole way of living. By allowing God to do for me what I could not do for myself, I found a Jesus full of grace and mercy who changed my life forever.

Praise God there is a church like Serenity that identifies Jesus as the way to find that spiritual love we have all been seeking. God is our strength and our refuge!

Please share on how you have realized God is doing for you what you could not do for yourself.

I'm Cyndy. Thanks for letting me chair the meeting.

OTHER SHARES AND TOPICS

SELF-PRESERVATION
Jennifer (Horton) Michie, September 2012

I'm Jennifer, and I'm an Overcomer.

Today I want to share with you an excerpt from my journal as a topic for sharing:

> Is self-preservation the first law of Nature? Why, then, does Greed urge you to self-sacrifice in order only to achieve his aim of hurting your brothers? (Kahlil Gibran)

I have been pondering self-preservation for many years. I realize that it is my concept of this that is wounding me. If self-preservation is human nature, why does it lead me into self-destruction? In efforts to protect myself, I must turn on my brother and fall out of love which, in fact, fails to preserve my innermost self. I am trapped in a false understanding of what my innermost self truly is.

My innermost self is the pure part of me that loves deeply and is humble and vulnerable and child-like. The fortified wall of fear has its warriors standing guard around this tender center of self—the self that is hidden in Christ with God and that sees beauty, and love, and forgiveness. The self that is safely inside the kingdom of heaven.

The kingdom of heaven continues to suffer violence. The outer shell of fear attempts to protect it from the violence, but in its attempt to do so robs the expression and expansion of this kingdom within.

I am shackled by this dichotomy. In so many ways I am, in fact, aiding and abetting the enemy of myself rather than protecting myself. In so doing, it is me that is being divided.

Father, set me free. Set me free from fear's promise of pain. This fear of suffering causes me more suffering than the "warriors" of judgment, criticism, bitterness, control, etc. are protecting me from. By rejecting others, I am rejecting my own salvation.

> Above all else, guard your heart,
>   for everything you do flows from it (Proverbs 4:23).

True "self-preservation" lies in the above. To truly preserve myself, I must keep my heart free from bitterness, resentment, unforgiveness, jealousy, malice, and all that would seek to harden it. The harder it becomes, the more breakable it is.

I'm Jennifer. Thanks for letting me chair the meeting.

Take-A-Ways
Linda Widhalm, February 2013

Earlier this week I was having dinner with my sister and her husband when, quite unexpectedly, my brother-in-law thanked me for what I had shared with him at a previously shared meal. At the previous meal they were struggling with how to handle some situations with their adult son and were quite openly sharing and looking for some help. I did quite a bit of 12th Stepping. After all, dealing with my own son is how and why I entered through the door of Overcomers for the first time.

My brother-in-law ended with tears in his eyes as he said, "There were quite a few take-a-ways." Take-a-ways are those things that have a lasting affect, have been significant or stuck with us. Since that meal, I have been pondering take-a-ways in my life. I thought tonight we could share with each other some of our take-a-ways. I will start.

In a meeting, Angela said, just as part of her share, "I've learned that everything that happens to me isn't about me." It has been several years since I heard those words. I do not remember ever hearing them before that meeting. I do not know anything else Angela said that night, but those words have stuck with me. I find myself at times reassessing some of my life events in light of that truth.

For instance, say a person comes home in a bad mood, the dog bounds over to say hello and instead of getting their head petted gets kicked across the floor. Is that about the dog? No. The person took out their anger over something or someone else on the dog. What if for the rest of his life the dog believed he was worthless, unloved, ugly, less than or different than other dogs because of that one event? How tragic!

I have had some bad things happened to me because I was in the wrong place at the wrong time, too. Those are not about me, so, I have given myself a break over some of those things. I have given God a break over those things. Along the way it has helped me to not take a lot of other things personally, too.

Tell us one of your take-a-ways.

My name is Linda. Thanks for letting me chair the meeting.

Look What You've Done for Me
Jason Kelley, 2013

My name is Jason. I'm an overcomer.

Recently I was thinking about everything God has done for me since I turned my will and my life over to Him and worked the Steps. This song came from thinking about Him, about what He has done for me, and about what I still need Him to do for me.

Look What You've Done
by Jason Kelley

VERSE:

Give me courage to stand against my enemies,
Give me strength to endure the front lines,
Give me faith that defeats all my unbelief,
For You are God,
You are good,
and I am Yours.

CHORUS:

I know that Satan's gonna try
to crush my heart and close my eyes;
But I will look to You,
I will run to You.
I'm not a sinner in disguise,
I'm a sinner that's alive,
And I will carry my cross no matter the cost.
Look what You've done for me.

(return to the verse and repeat)

In gratitude to God, and for the sake of those who came here needing to hear some experience, strength, and hope, let's share what God has done in each of our lives as a result of working the Steps. Thanks for letting me share the words of this song. And thanks for letting me chair the meeting tonight.

TWO VOICES
Jennifer (Horton) Michie

A pastor shared his perception of the two voices.

> The voice of our Enemy feels like a cattle prod or a whip, he said, using fear to drive us. The voice of Love draws us.

> The voice of the Enemy is behind us pushing us. The Voice of Love is in front of us beckoning us to follow.

> The voice behind demands. The Voice in front invites.

> The voice behind drives us out. The Voice in front welcomes us in.

> The voice behind tears us down. The Voice in front builds us up, gives us strength and courage.

One of the biggest struggles in my life is which voice to listen to. Everybody has a certain expectation of what my life should look like. I am learning it is not theirs to decide. I am my Beloved's and He is mine. Jesus said "My sheep know My voice and will not listen to the voice of the stranger." I find great freedom in God's permission to reject the voice of the stranger no matter how seemingly "accurate" his words.

For me, the difference in His voice and the voice of the stranger is Love. A pastor of mine once said, "Truth divorced from the heart of Love fails as truth." It does not matter if the words are accurate; if those words are not carried in Love, they will fail to do what truth is designed to do: set me free.

Truth outside of the loving heart of God will tear down and destroy. Truth that is saturated in Love may cut deep, but the cut is designed to clear out the space for Love to heal. The stranger has no love for me. The stranger may say he loves me, but my heart knows when it is loved. When someone has a judgment or a criticism of me, I filter it through how loved I feel by that person. The ones who criticize me the most are often the ones who know me the least; or, the ones who have chosen to know me only based on my shortcomings, real or presumed. The heart decides.

I have found the heart of God (Love) in someone upon first meeting them, and I have found the "stranger" in someone I have known for years. I have also found both in each. It is a moment by moment distinction because God uses whomever He decides to use in order to keep my trust in Him and not in a person. He is training me to hear

Him wherever He may be. Once I know His voice regardless of the face, I will no longer rely on man.

My name is Jennifer. Thanks for letting me chair.

Relapse
Mac Martin, 2015

My problem is Mac, and alcohol makes it worse. "The same person will drink again." Alcoholism is not only a disease it is a symptom of a need for a new design for living.

After working the Steps and having a spiritual awakening, we humbly ask God to remove our desire to drink. Then we are not cured but we are reprieved, daily contingent on the maintenance of our spiritual condition. If we pray daily, go to as many meetings as possible, and work with others, we increase our ability to stay sober and we become a new person. However, if we let up on our spiritual program of action and rest on our laurels, we are headed for trouble. We start slipping back into our old way of thinking and we start becoming the old person we used to be. We are in grave danger of drinking again.

I have been sober since April 24, 2004. When I miss going to a lot of meetings and I start running the show instead of letting God do it, I slowly go back to my old way of thinking without realizing it. I am fortunate to have a wife who somehow stayed with me through forty-five years of drinking, and she knows the demeanor of the "same man I used to be." She will remind me that I need to go to more meetings when she sees me heading in the wrong direction. And I never argue because I know she is right.

If you do not work with others and you are not surrounded by good people that love you and are willing to help you, like a sponsor, or you do not have the ability to stay involved in your own recovery, you are in danger of becoming "that same person" again and relapse.

If you have identified pitfalls that can lead to relapse in your life, please share them with us.

Thanks for letting me chair the meeting.

SHARE: *Road to Relapse* by Cyndy Sanders, 2015

I'm Cyndy, and I'm an Overcomer.

I started drinking at the age of 13 and decided then it was the perfect solution to my insecurity, anger, and anxiety. By the time I had graduated from college, my life with alcohol had also graduated from beer and wine to whiskey and tequila. Alcohol had become my best friend and my worst enemy.

Eventually my friends intervened and made the appointment for me to go into the hospital. I left the clinic after two weeks, "scared straight," got into AA, and did not touch a drop of alcohol for 16 years. I was convinced then I would never drink again.

AA, which I believe was divinely inspired, is an excellent prescription for staying sober. But I became complacent and stopped chairing and sharing in meetings. It got to the point where I was no longer reading the literature or doing service work, and I failed to get a new sponsor when mine moved. Yet, when I picked up my 16 year chip, I was certain I would never drink again. In fact, I had gotten quite cocky about it.

During this time I also attended several Overcomers meetings, but it was too little, too late. When my husband and I celebrated our anniversary, I suggested we get a bottle of champagne and *not* tell anyone. He was totally against this, but I insisted. You probably know how it turned out. Within a week, I was back to seriously drinking. In six months I landed in the hospital again.

When I returned to AA, I was made to feel very welcome. But I also remembered you nice people in Overcomers, and once I came back I knew I would never be alone again. You are like my family. For me, the emphasis on Jesus Christ as my Higher Power was the missing piece. Looking back, I can see the road to my relapse included:

- Mentally—blaming others for my alcoholism, not wanting the stigma of saying I was an alcoholic, and thinking celebrations need alcohol;
- Spiritually—not being connected to Jesus Christ as my Higher Power; and
- Physically—not staying under the care of a sponsor, and not attending meetings regularly.

I will be picking up my nine year chip soon. All glory be to God!

Thanks for letting me share.

Forgiveness, A Pleasing Aroma
Linda Widhalm, May 2015

I'm Linda, and I'm an Overcomer.

If you are like me, you have to ask God every single day for forgiveness for something. And every single day He forgives. If you are like me, you have to forgive someone else for something they did today that hurt you or for something done in the past that reared its ugly head. Old offenses, even those we have forgiven before, have a way of breaking through to the present to hurt us again and need a fresh round of forgiveness.

If you are like me, this constant forgiveness thing can seem like such a drudgery! I recently realized I have been thinking of it all wrong! I eat everyday. I definitely drink coffee and water everyday. I breathe all day and all night. There are many healthy, helpful, even vital things I do for me everyday. I need to think of my forgiving others as equally vital to my daily life as these things, because it is!

Forgiveness was in a category for me like going to the dentist, getting an immunization, washing dishes, doing laundry, taking out the trash. However, forgiveness belongs in a category like smelling a flower, watching a sunset, hearing a child laugh, getting good news, seeing an old friend, getting a hug. Or, better yet, like winning the lottery and being able to share it with others everyday. Some quotations I meditated on helped me come to this conclusion. Listen to this one:

> The true Christian is like sandalwood which imparts its fragrance to the axe which cuts it without doing any harm in return.
> -Sadu Sundar Singh

Kathleen Dillard says, forgiveness is not natural; it is supernatural, so we must ask God for His supernatural power. Only God can turn doing work into giving gifts!

I'm Linda. Thanks for letting me chair the meeting.

SHARE: My name's Che', Overcomer.

In Step 10 it says we take a personal inventory and when we were wrong we promptly admit it. This Step helps us to take a look at ourselves every day. When did someone else hurt me? Or when did I hurt some else today? What should I have done instead of what I did?

A lot of the time before you are able to get to the forgiveness part, you must see your part. Once you see that you have something to be forgiven for then it is easier to forgive—most of the time.

> For if you forgive other people when they sin against you, your heavenly Father will also forgive you (Matthew 6:14).

Thanks for letting me share.

SHARE: *Love Her* by Aunt Laurie, February 2013

Hi. My name is Aunt Laurie, and I'm an Overcomer.

Some things were shared in Overcomers tonight which got me thinking about a testimony I think should be shared here.

Many years ago I was the parent of a very difficult and destructive child. Her behavior was horrible and I was constantly called to the school for problems. We were asked to (please) not return to a church our family had attended because of her out-of-control behavior. I thought we were doing everything "right" by the Bible, and yet the behavior problems were just getting worse.

One night in desperation I cried out to God that I was at the end of my rope and needed answers. I sensed the Lord speaking to my heart: "Love her."

I thought that was odd because *of course* I loved her. I prayed again. And again I heard, "Love her like you are *in love* with her."

I began to think of the way I would treat someone I was *in love* with— listening with rapt attention; gazing into their eyes; being happy to be in their presence; praising them; being patient, kind; recognizing their strengths; giving the benefit of the doubt when things go wrong. I realized I was so focused on controlling the behavior of my daughter to stop the public embarrassment that our every interaction was nothing but critical judgment.

As I began to demonstrate my deep love for my daughter and teach her strategies to learn to control herself instead of me trying to control and criticize her every action and idea, the Lord worked on her heart and she had a miraculous conversion at the age of 13. She was still strong-willed, but our troubles and painful conflict were over.

My daughter is a beautiful woman now with children of her own, and she is the pride of my life. Parents, here is my best advice: Ditch the criticism; demonstrate the love; pray like crazy.

I'm Auntie Laurie. Thanks for letting me share.

SHARE: *Putting the World Back Together* by Mac Martin, April 2014

My problem is Mac and alcohol makes it worse.

I heard the story of a father who needed to keep his son busy for a little while so he picked up a magazine with a picture of the world on the front. He ripped off the cover, tore it into little pieces, then gave the boy a roll of tape and instructed him to put the picture back together again. In what seemed like no time at all the boy proudly presented the picture of the world all put back together! The father, amazed, asked his son how he had done it so fast. The boy said, "Well, I saw the back of the picture before you tore it up. It was a picture of a man. I thought it was easier so I turned the pieces over. Once I had the man put back together, the world was put together, too!"

I am very grateful I have been sober for [# of days], and so are a lot of other people. I'm Mac. Thanks for letting me share.

SHARE: *Humility* by Jennifer (Horton) Michie

My name is Jennifer and I'm an Overcomer.

I think it takes more humility to unlearn than it does to learn. To know something is black and white gives a strong sense of security. It is a lot easier to free-fall with a broken parachute than it is to go without one.

I had relied many years on a broken gospel and expected it to save me. What I found was that I was already saved.

I'm Jennifer. Thanks for letting me share.

SHARE: An Original Poem by Mac Martin

To The Agnostic

Lift up your eyes on high, and behold who hath created these things (Isaiah 40:26a KJV).

There are no miracles in things that we can explain,
We control and command the things we are able to explain,
Therefore it is human nature to seek to explain;
Without God life makes no sense,
If there were no God we would be accidents;
We would exist in the universe by random chance,
Life would have no purpose, meaning or significance;

While we are here on earth there would be no right or wrong,
And no hope for eternity after we are gone;
You should correctly use your starved imagination,
To observe and behold all of God's creation;
See the wind that blows every day and every night,
Every sign of the sky, every beast, and every mite;
Every flower that blooms and every flower that withers,
Every small creek, and all the magnificent rivers;
If you believe in God, nature is a sacred observance,
He will come to you if you realize His omnipotence;
Is your starved imagination focused on an idol forever?
Is that idol yourself? Your work? Or your conception of another?
If so, your imagination of God will be starved,
    and you have no power
When you have difficulties to endure in your darkest hour.

Thanks for letting me share what came out of my daily meditation. My problem is Mac and alcohol makes it worse.

SHARE: *Relationships* by Jennifer (Horton) Michie

My name is Jennifer, and I'm an Overcomer. [Hi, Jennifer!]

When we build relationships with one another, we often, unintentionally perhaps, lay the foundation of that relationship on "thou shalts" and "thou shalt nots" rather than simply on "Love God and love one another." We adhere to a behavioral code that we have decided is acceptable, and we withdraw love from each other when the behavioral code we have set in place is not followed. We have our beliefs that drinking, smoking, adultery, being out of church/meetings, etc. is wrong and therefore we withdraw love from those who are committing those infractions.

When I was dealing with some pretty serious issues in my own life, I remember thinking as I reflected on the people in my life, "I see their love for marriage, church/meetings, the Bible, the program, etc., but I don't see their love for *me*."

While, undoubtedly, there is a place for appropriate boundaries in order to keep our own heart free to love, Love, nonetheless, remains the highest call. The boundaries I set must be for the purpose of keeping my heart free from negativity and able to love the one I am struggling to understand.

For example, if being near "Sally" keeps me stirred up in negativity and judgment, then I may have to create space—maybe even just for a season—from Sally. However, the distance should not communicate that Sally is bad and unworthy of being loved. I have no obligation or permission to judge Sally. My judgment is to be on my own heart. I can and should judge the condition of my own heart and decide what triggers the things I do not want within me for my own personal health. My love for people should far outweigh my love for principals.

Ultimately, I am responsible for my *own* recovery. My own recovery is contingent upon my ability to give and receive Love and keep myself from things that wound my own soul. The more Love is able to dwell in my heart, the better my chances are of staying out of harmful behaviors that cause me to relapse into the thing I am seeking freedom from. Judgment of my fellow man and the corresponding withdrawal of love is not conducive to my recovery. Contempt for another will not make room for my own progress.

Thanks for letting me share.

SHARE: *Fruit* by Jennifer (Horton) Michie

My name is Jennifer, and I'm an Overcomer. [Hi, Jennifer!]

Fruit is a difficult thing to assess because it takes time to bud, ripen, and be truly satisfying. I have often had others judge me, or I have attempted to judge myself, based on "fruit" or lack thereof.

When we come into rooms like this, most of us are in deep pain and turmoil. Our lives are full of chaos. Just because that is where we are today does not mean our whole lives have been that way. Fruit production is subject to the elements, the seed, water supply, soil, seasons, and so forth.

Many times I have been disappointed in myself because I was not seeing a lot of fruit in my life. I guess, ultimately, I was not living up to my own expectations. God said that I would be "like a tree planted by the water" and that I would bear fruit in "due season" (Psalm 1:3). It is very difficult when others think (or I think) that I should be producing a certain fruit which I can't seem to produce no matter how hard I try. It is especially hard when it's winter.

I am learning to have patience with myself and let the seasons of my life come and go. Fruit is God's to define and God's to produce. I am God's garden and He is the Master Gardener. He is cultivating the crop He desires my life to produce. As I focus on who He is and trust that He loves me and that everything He is doing in my life is springing forth from that Love—not from my deserving of it—then I do not have to worry about fruit or any other element of my growth process. I surrender and trust that He Who began a good work in me will complete it until the end (Philippians 1:6). I trust that God knows the exact way to accomplish *His* goals in my life.

Winter has just as much value in the life of a tree as does spring. In the winter, the tree sheds its leaves and all of its energy is focused on digging deep for water. As the tree suffers from its journey for water, it has nothing left to give in the way of producing leaves and fruit. It is a necessary part of its life cycle. The roots become stronger through this season, therefore, the fruit and leaves are much healthier in their season.

I am learning to stop expecting my life to be full of big, beautiful displays of external health during the painful, dry seasons. Rather than hating myself or trying to hang plastic fruit on myself, I embrace the pain, search for water, and know that spring will come in time. I keep putting one foot in front of the other. I do not surrender to the judgment of man on my external life but continue to surrender to the One Who knows me well and calls me by name and is taking special and tender care of me every minute of every day.

Thanks for letting me share.

BIRTHDAY NIGHT SHARE: *Second Chances* by Mac Martin, April 25, 2016 (his 11th Brithday)

My problem is Mac and alcohol makes it worse.

Second Chances

My God is awesome in every way
He always forgives me every day
When I repeat my sins, and my shame is immense
He always gives me, another "second chance"

My God is the God of second chances
He forgives all of my offenses
When I do the same things all over again
He opens His arms, and take me back in
I don't know why He doesn't turn me away
When I ask for another "second chance" everyday
I guess it's because as He watches from above
He smiles down at us, with an undying love

As I recall my sins that I have done today
I wonder why I choose to live that way
Oh what can I do, I am in a guilty trance
I know, I'll ask God for another "second chance"

I am glad I've been sober for 11 years; so are a lot of other people. When I was born, God gave me a gift: Free Will. Eleven years ago when I started working the Steps, I gave it back. I use page 25 of the *Big Book* kinda like a creed. I changed all the pronouns to make it personal. It goes like this:

> There is a solution. I didn't like the self-searching, the leveling of my pride, the confession of shortcomings which the process requires for its successful consummation. But I saw that it really worked in others, and I had come to believe in the hopelessness and futility of life as I had been living it. When, therefore, I was approached by those in whom the problem had been solved, there was nothing left for me but to pick up the simple kit of spiritual tools laid at my feet. I have found much of heaven and I have been rocketed into a fourth dimension of existence of which I had not even dreamed.

> The great fact is this, and nothing less: That I have had deep and effective spiritual experiences which have revolutionized my whole attitude toward life, toward my fellows, and toward God's universe. The central fact of my life today is the absolute certainty that my Creator has entered into my heart and life in a way which is indeed miraculous. He has commenced to accomplish those things for me which I could never do by myself.

I'm Mac. Thanks for letting me share.

Section 3

SERENITY CHURCH
POWER FOR THE POWERLESS

A Saturday Night Church

The rich and poor meet together:
the LORD is the maker of them all.

Proverbs 22:2 KJV

Every time I come through the doors
of Serenity Church
I feel like I won the lottery!

Rachel M., May 22, 2004

What We Do and Why We Do It

WHAT'S THE BIG IDEA? The concept of a church where folks in recovery would feel comfortable to gather together for worship and recovery in the same place was conceived by the Holy Spirit, grew in the heart of John Featherston and, well, you can read all about it in his book *Never Alone Again*.

What we will discuss in the coming pages is the *who, what, where, when, how,* and *whys* we do what we do to make Serenity Church happen each week, as well as some of the pitfalls. We are hopeful what you read here allows you to learn from our mistakes and helps you find and focus on your own mission.

Serenity Church does not function like most churches, does not have the same goals as most churches, and does not measure success by the same standards. These are important things to understand before venturing out to begin a Serenity Church.

LEADERSHIP TEAM

Serenity Churches are begun and run by a small group of people who have reached a point of stability (whatever that is) in their recovery lives. Really, that means as individuals they have come to accept their strengths and weaknesses. The team is successful because we are willing to work together so each one is filling a role which uses their strengths and relies on other team members in areas of weakness. We know this because we have been broken and pieced back together at least once already.

Our core leadership is via our Leadership Team (LT—we tried to call ourselves Deacons but it hasn't stuck). The LT is made up of four couples: the pastor and his wife (the voice of experience), the music minister and his wife (the voice of compassion), the treasurer and his wife (the voice of reason), and the business man and his wife (the voice of insight). Some on the LT have experience and training in Biblical studies, teaching, and church ministry while others have not even walked into the doors of a school of higher learning (Okay, so there is only one of those. Me). Some on the LT have experience, training, and common sense regarding finances while others willingly acknowledge that field is a weakness for them. Some have experience and training in business, or the law, or counseling. All have spiritual gifts that operate within the team. And all have learned valuable lessons in the school of hard knocks.

All business and financial decisions of the church are handled by the LT in closed (used loosely), weekly (used loosely) dinner meetings. We eat together and fellowship over the meal then discuss church business, pray about business, discuss issues that have arisen, pray about those issues, pass resolutions, share our visions for the future, report back on assignments, etc. We do not make any decisions that are not unanimous. We give ourselves and each other time to process, pray, and meditate so we do not rush into rash decisions or fall into disharmony with each other.

As you can imagine, this church is made up of people just climbing out of a deep, dark pit who have so many other things to deal with without wondering how their rent is going to be paid—at church. Many are trying to pay *last* month's rent at home. Many of the people in the pews are struggling for their next meal. Most are very generous with what little they have because they have been so much lower in the past and want to offer to others the help given to them. Their resources are meager, but they give from what they have. It is not always money. They give their time and service to each other freely.

We remind ourselves frequently that addictions stunt maturity. If an individual began using as a teenager, when the fog of addiction begins to lift they may possibly still be a teenager emotionally, or socially, etc. We must be patient with them—and help them to be patient with themselves as they face the challenges of adjusting to the real world.

RECOVERY LEADERSHIP TEAM

We have found that once lives are stabilized and restored, a certain percentage of folks move on to mainstream churches. Another percentage were not ready to leave their addiction and disappear for a while, then maybe show up again. Others are called to stay at Serenity Church and serve.

Some of those who stay may be asked to serve on what we call the Recovery Leadership Team (RLT). The RLT meets regularly to discuss what is working with church meetings and what is not. The RLT divides up responsibilities for finding volunteers to chair meetings, give communion meditations, set up rooms, put out signs, make coffee, clean up, etc. When the RLT encounters a problem or has new ideas, they are shared with the LT at our joint monthly dinner Breakfast-Palooza meeting (Yes, this dinner is made up of a pot-luck of breakfast foods). The LT measures the problems and RLT's ideas against the instructions of Jesus to love and help hurting folks, the goals of Serenity Church, and the yardstick of our previous hard-knocks education.

Because of the good work of our RLT, many complicated issues have been made much easier, new groups of hurting people needing help have been identified, and the RLT has kept the four LT couples from burning out! Together we have also avoided falling into old pits again.

THE TIES WE MAKE

Needless to say, Serenity Church would not exist if it were not for the tithes of a core group of people plus generous donations from outside sources. Those outside sources are individuals who, for a variety of reasons, understand the need for Serenity Church. Maybe a struggling loved one was helped by Serenity Church; maybe they lost a loved one to addiction; or maybe they, them self, were once helped by Serenity Church or its ministries. Some are folks who see God is working here and choose to join Him in this work. Whatever their reasons, we could not function without them. They are vital. We frequently thank God for them and ask Him to bless them in their lives and work. And we frequently ask God to raise up additional generous folks.

Serenity Church has partnered with brothers and sisters in Christ from every denomination, creed, and social class to reach those in need of recovery. Those in need of recovery have come out of every denomination, creed, and social class.

WE DO NOT MEASURE SUCCESS BY A GROWING MEMBERSHIP

As a matter of fact, we do not have membership. We are interested in providing a place where families can worship together during a difficult time in their lives. People come, people go. We are not interested in nurturing in them a commitment to us as individuals or to Serenity Church. We are interested in nurturing in them a revelation of the unconditional love of God and giving their Higher Power a name: Jesus Christ. What happens as a result of that, we pray, will happen as God wills it.

Many people drive long distances to attend Serenity Church. They sacrifice time and money to do so because they are in desperate need.

It is not feasible, however, for these folks to make this sacrifice forever, and it is much better for them to get well and then carry the message to their circles of influence where they live. Frequently, former attendees come back with a friend at their side who needs what we have to give. After a few weeks that friend begins coming on their own.

> Just one day of being at your church has made an impact on my life in a major way. I always felt I had done too much wrong to be saved. Your church has shown me that through our Lord Jesus Christ I will be saved! Thank you for caring! — Ryan H.

WE BAPTIZE

Like Jesus, we do not worry about the worthiness of the one performing the baptism. Jesus went to his cousin, John. Usually the one desiring baptism inquires of their sponsor how to go about it, or they seek out someone who has helped them understand Jesus as their Higher Power. That is the person they usually want to have baptize them, so that is who does it.

We have had as many as four different people baptizing in one night. Sometimes one is not comfortable doing the baptizing, so they climb in and assist. Sometimes others stand with them but outside the baptistry. This is made easier since we use a round, portable baptistry which is easily assembled, disassembled, and stored.

WE CELEBRATE

Every year on the anniversary of the first-ever Serenity Church worship service, we celebrate our Sereniversary! Our first service was on Pentecost weekend, so we celebrate on the Saturday of Pentecost each year. We invite everyone we know to come join us in celebrating and thanking God for the work He is doing in and through us. We cannot do what we do without many brothers and sister in Christ holding us up in prayer and financially supporting us, so we ask them to come celebrate, too!

Folks come from even farther away than usual to take part. We cancel Overcomers for just this one night a year and have a fellowship with finger foods after the worship time.

The youth celebrate with us. The teachers prepare a party for the kids.

> I'm glad I came. You all are truly doing the Lord's work, and it was a great Sereniversary for me. You should do something

to tone down the enthusiasm that pastor has for the Lord!
— MCPO Steve Hines, USCG (ret)

We Dedicate Babies and Children to the Lord

When parents in recovery come to understand their responsibility to raise their children to know God and His Son, Jesus Christ, they often ask to dedicate their children. Serenity Church is a family. Their kids are our kids. When we do this we join the parents in this occasion and promise that we will consider their children as our children and share in this responsibility and dedication.

We Recognize the Hard Days and Seasons

Folks in recovery usually have a hard time with holidays. Either they have trouble due to lack of family, or they struggle with the probability of alcohol and/or abusers being present at family gatherings.

Especially in the beginning, folks need a safe place to be and an opportunity to make good memories. This is discussed in the Overcomers Section of this book, but it is important to mention it here, as well. We make a priority of celebrating and educating, as a church, regarding the spiritual significance of Christian holidays while, at the same time, identifying that many dangers and pitfalls exist for folks in recovery.

We have chosen, as a church, not to emphasize Mother's Day and Father's Day. Reasons for feeling pain on those days are vast and deep. Our compassion is essential to our mission of providing a grace-filled place to meet our Higher Power, Jesus.

We Have Seasons of Prayer

Approximately every other year, whenever the Lord leads, we have a season of prayer, usually lasting a month or more and using the Serenity Church Prayer. We use a bracelet of beads to keep us on track in our praying for Serenity Church, ourselves, our family members, and anyone else the Lord prompts us to pray for on a daily basis. *Much* has happened in individual lives, and in the church as a whole, as a result of these seasons of prayer.

To hear the sermon kicking off a season of prayer, go on-line to The Serenity Church Home Page: www.serenitychurch.net; or in the Serenity Church App:

Choose: Messages of Hope
then choose: 40 Days of Serenity
then choose: "What I Heard in the Desert"

You may choose to fast-forward through the first six minutes, or go straight to the meat of the message at the 13-minute mark.

The lesson explains each piece of this spiritual exercise:

The power of persistent prayer — Luke 11:5-13
Jesus as healer — Matthew 9:9-13
        of our minds — Romans 12:1-2
        of our hearts — Matthew 5:8
        and our bodies — Romans 7:15 - 8:2

OUTLINE FOR OUR PRAYING

Declaration: "Jesus is Lord. Jesus is Lord. Jesus is Lord. Jesus is Lord. Jesus is Lord" (Philippians 2:5-11, Luke 11:2).

Large Bead– Pray the Serenity Prayer:

God grant me the serenity to accept the things I cannot change,
    Courage to change the things I can,
    And wisdom to know the difference.

Each small bead: Pray the Serenity Church Prayer:

        Father, please show us what we're missing.
        Father, please give us what we're missing.
        Heal our hearts, our minds, and our bodies
            through Christ.

End with the large bead: Pray the Serenity Prayer.

Where We Do What We Do

WE DO NOT MEASURE SUCCESS BY BUILDINGS OR PROGRAMS

That's right. We do not measure success by building buildings or running a lot of programs. We rent space in already-built buildings and use them during hours the building is normally idle. This enables us to focus our limited funds, manpower, and other resources on the people who are hurting.

We abide by the policies set in place by our host church or ministry for building use or childcare. We keep it simple. We have found that when we do not keep it simple, problems arise which distract us and take our focus away from our goals of helping the specific people group we have been called to minister to. In short, if the church down the street is doing it, there may be no need for us to do it, too.

That does not, however, keep us from joining them in those tasks, activities, or ministries. Folks in recovery need to stay busy doing good work, enjoying good fellowship, and helping others who need help. Some churches and ministries will partner with us for specific long-term or short-term projects or events such as: getting kids to summer camps or Vacation Bible School, assisting in tornado relief, feeding the homeless, or holding holiday services.

And when one of their folks needs recovery, they call us. We have recovery programs, understanding of addictions, and a different way of thinking about helping hurting people.

Currently we have four Overcomers groups in two locations within The Colony, Texas. An additional group meets outside of The Colony: Serenity Church–Metro (not to be confused with the organization Metro Relief, below). Each Saturday morning around 25 folks board the Metro Relief bus and head to South Dallas, taking breakfast and groceries and holding an Overcomers meeting and a recovery worship service for folks in the Cooper Street area. Sunlight Missionary Baptist Church has partnered with both Metro Relief and Serenity Church to make this happen. Sunlight provides the building, Metro Relief provides hot meals, clothing donations, and other assistance. We provide worship and recovery assistance.

PLACES WE FREQUENT

It is also essential our folks continue to participate in another 12 Step meeting for the interaction which occurs there—participating through sharing and sponsoring. This helps provide a constant flow of people into Overcomers and Serenity Church.

Another reason for our folks to attend other 12 Step groups is so we can keep our finger on the pulse of the current recovery community.

A third reason is so we will not forget where we once were. Listening to the stories of those fresh into recovery is essential to stave off possible self-denial of our own "incomprehensible demoralization."

But possibly the most important reason to attend other groups is the stories we can share of our experience, of what gave us strength and the hope we now have, stories which bring hope to those still struggling. Every meeting attended is both an opportunity to get something we need to hear and to give something someone else needs to hear.

testimonies /stories

How We Do What We Do

THE LANGUAGE WE SPEAK

At Serenity Church we have found it imperative that we speak recovery—not church, not churchy recovery, not psycho babble. When folks walk through the doors feeling alone, afraid, or vulnerable and they hear familiar things like the Serenity Prayer or the 12 Steps being said by people who look, well, rather common, they begin to feel comfortable.

Every angel visitation story in the Bible begins with "Do not be afraid!" because fear clogs our ears and deceives our eyes. Those Bible stories do not give us the time lag between the angel saying not to be afraid and when the angel actually delivered the message. There was at least a short gap of time not recorded there. We can shorten the gap between the ears-clogged-with-fear time and the hearing-of-the-message time by speaking recovery language—the language of *The Big Book of Alcoholics Anonymous*, the language they are familiar with from their 12 Step group.

WE DO NOT JUDGE

It is the Holy Spirit's job to convict, God's job to judge, and my job to love. ~ Billy Graham

Folks come to us with all sorts of marital issues, living arrangements, sexual orientations, major and minor addictions (i.e., tobacco), vocabularies, body art, and you name it. We find that if we take them just as they are and stay focused on what God has given us to do, some of those things will get sorted out later if and when God prompts them. It is not our business. Our business is, like the prophet Isaiah wrote, to "Feed the hungry, and help those in trouble. ... Then your light will shine out from the darkness, and the darkness around you will be as bright as noonday" (adapted from Isaiah 58). Our focus is not on bringing light. Our focus is on feeding the hungry both physically and spiritually and on helping those in trouble. The light dawning is a promised result when we do what God says. We see it over and over again. Like Che', our recovery pastor, says, "There's nothing like watching the light come on in their eyes!"

We do not even judge one another when one has to change their sobriety date. We do not focus on the fall, we focus on the getting back up—and on the progress.

WE DO NOT CHASE THOSE WHO LEAVE

People only get and keep recovery when they desperately *want* recovery, not when they desperately *need* recovery. Chasing folks who have changed their mind and "gone back out" is a waste of energy. Chasing folks can just make them run away farther and faster. Chasing folks tends to close our door of ministry to them. We stay available for when they *want* to come back.

WE GET THEM TO RECOVERY

Our recovery pastor transports folks to inpatient recovery, or meets them there, helps them get checked in, prepares them and their loved ones for what to expect, plus many other components involved in assisting people into recovery. He holds their hand through the process, but it takes tough love.

The first time in recovery does not always stick, so he takes them again when they are ready and ask for help. The stories are numerous and amazing on developing relationships with folks, getting them to recovery, and reuniting them with family members who have not seen them in years.

WE PROVIDE A PLACE FOR SMOKERS TO SMOKE

That's it. We do.

How We Deal with Our Children

SERENITY KIDS BEDTIME PRAYER
Linda Widhalm

Dear Jesus, thank You for today,
For home and school and work and play
Thank You for my family,
And my church that brings Serenity
Be with those I love and miss [name them]
Give them each a holy kiss
While I sleep please heal my heart
And every other wounded part
'Cuz You are Lord, Amen

People were bringing little children to Jesus for Him to place His hands on them, but the disciples rebuked them.

When Jesus saw this, He was indignant. He said to them, "Let the little children come to Me, and do not hinder them, for the kingdom of God belongs to such as these" (Mark 10:13-14).

YOUR KID IS OUR KID

We emphasize this belief when we dedicate our children, too. The Gospel writers agree that Jesus welcomed the children, laid His hands on them and blessed them. We welcome and bless our kids, too. And we find they bless us right back!

WE HAVE A PAID STAFF OF ADULT TEACHERS

This paid staff is aided by a seasoned volunteer. We also have a few available substitutes for the teachers. Our children have experienced enough instability in their homes in the past, so we try to give them stability by having the same teacher each week.

Teachers communicate with parents in the worship service by text messaging if a problem arises. Many folks who attend services with their children do not have enough recovery yet to help as a volunteer.

We may call folks that help "volunteers" but we *ask* them to volunteer when we see they are both ready and gifted to help.

Parents and children worship together until a certain point in the service (after communion, before the sermon) when the children are dismissed to class. This gives teachers an opportunity to worship in the congregation, too. We try to schedule special events like baptisms before communion so the kids and teachers do not miss out.

Teachers for the littlest ones—birth through age 3 or 4 years—receive children beginning 10 minutes before services start. These teachers do not have an opportunity to worship with us, so we hire women who attend a Sunday church.

During the Worship Service

Children are divided, generally, by age as the teachers see fit. We do not use dated materials. Our classes for children under eight years old use *Leading Little Ones to God* by Marian M. Schoolland (may now be out of print; ours was bought, used, from Amazon.com). There are 86 lessons which the teachers adapt to the ability of their class. By the time they begin the book again, the children attending are not the same ones any more, keeping it simple. Substitute teachers only need to know which lesson to use.

We have been blessed with teachers for our older children who have been creative and adapted other books and methods to teach Bible basics with little expense. God has provided us with great teachers with hearts full of love for the kids. We pray for them. We appreciate them. Our parents and kids love and appreciate them.

The materials and snacks for these classes are funded by some of what comes in through the Overcomers offering.

During the Overcomers Hour

The youngest children may be taken to play in the nursery while the older ones gather in one room for crafts and games. Not everyone attending service stays for Overcomers, so the crowd dwindles. Volunteer teachers are dismissed. If the remaining children are very few, a paid teacher may have the blessing of attending Overcomers.

DURING WEEKDAY OVERCOMERS MEETINGS

We do not generally provide childcare for meetings held during the week. Folks can usually find someone to care for their children for an hour. Since we have several meetings a week, spouses often alternate attendance at meetings; however, occasionally, we must consider the special needs of single parents and find a way to assist them in being able to attend.

> We did not start out with this method.
> We learned it in the school of hard knocks.

How We Deal with Our Teens

This was our greatest lesson to learn in the school of hard knocks. Leaving out how we learned our lessons, let me just tell you what decisions we made as a result of what we learned.

THREE RULES WE LIVE BY

1. Teens come to church and leave the church with their parents and attend youth class with their parents' permission.

2. Teens stay on the premises during church under their parents' supervision. If one slips out of the worship service without their parents noticing, the parent gets tapped to bring them back. If there is a problem during class, their parents are called to deal with it. If a teen comes with a friend, the friend's parents are responsible for them while they are in the worship service and in youth class.

3. Teens participate in all other church activities with their parents and under their parents' supervision.

We have not had problems since we began abiding by these three Rules and letting the teens in class discuss and create their own code of conduct. We have found that they call each other out when one is not abiding by their code.

Why solve problems
when you can operate in the solution?

YOUTH CODE OF CONDUCT

This is how we show respect to one another and to God.

1. We turn our phones off during class

2. We do not talk when someone else is talking

3. We do not gossip in class or about what happens in class; what happens in youth class, stays in youth class

4. We welcome the new person as the most important person in the room

We have a class for youth while their parents are in Overcomers so adults can be open and honest. That does not mean that teens who need recovery cannot attend Overcomers. Of course they can. That's what we're here for!

There are plenty of Sunday churches providing youth programs. Many of our folks attend a Sunday church as well as Serenity Church. There they can attend popular Bible studies, choirs, youth and children's programs, etc.

> *Author's Note*: The hardest part of getting this book published has been Serenity Church's constantly changing the way we do things in order to meet the needs of the folks currently attending, as well as their children and youth.
>
> As of May 2015 our youth class is run just like Overcomers. Once a month, the youth join with the Saturday night Overcomers group to celebrate Birthday Night where they receive monthly chips. Their leader arranges speaker meetings for them, too!

When We Do What We Do

SERENITY CHURCH IS A SATURDAY NIGHT CHURCH

Since evenings are when most folks have trouble not giving in to their addiction, and since most addicts would not be out of bed for a Sunday morning service, holding our worship service on Saturday evening is one way we provide what hurting folks need when they need it. For the alcoholic or the addict, the flow of the evening is designed to help provide a first day without drinking or using while they are surrounded by folks who know what they are going through.

TIME TABLE

4:00 - 6:00 No Regrets Praise Band and media folks set up and practice. Listeners welcome. (Coffee is started)

6:00 People begin arriving to set up for the evening
Helpers welcome

6:30 Slides begin running on the projection screen

Slides include welcome, announcements, names of those celebrating years of recovery for the month and how many years they are celebrating.

As they arrive, every newcomer is welcomed by a greeter, given a Welcome bag along with a bulletin. Our Welcome bag includes a Bible, a pen, a Serenity Church brochure, and a Serenity Church coin (see page 63).

6:55 Five-Minute Countdown on screen
Prayer huddle is formed by three to ten folks to pray for the service

7:00 Worship service starts

8:30 Worship service ends

When the worship service ends, a 10-minute countdown begins on the projection screen concluding with a slide that says: *"You're late!"*

8:45 - 9:45 Overcomers meeting and youth class

At 10 P.M. in our town an AA meeting begins right down the street. Newcomers to Serenity Church may be taken to that meeting by a recovery buddy or sponsor.

There it is! The possibility for seven hours in a row of prime time filled with welcomes, smiles, hugs, coffee making and coffee drinking, praise and worship, sharing and listening to others share, getting phone numbers of folks who know, praying the Serenity Prayer (3 times), reading the 12 Steps (3 times), reading the 12 Promises (3 times), praying the Lord's Prayer (3 times), followed by, "We're glad you came!" and finding out you are Never Alone Again.

What Our Worship Service Looks Like

Before the service begins, volunteers are selected (usually folks who showed up early) to do the readings and to serve communion.

Peppy Song

The band opens with a peppy song while those who have not found a seat yet get settled. The words are up on the projection screen. In the beginning we always started with "Lean On Me," a non-churchy song everyone had heard before.

Welcome, Moment of Silence, and Serenity Prayer

A seasoned Serenitarian welcomes everyone—and does a good, thorough job of it. Then they lead us in a moment of silence for those who still hurt, followed by the Serenity Prayer. The words are on the screen. We use the entire Serenity Prayer, not just the first verse.

Serenity Prayer
Reinhold Niebuhr (1892-1971)

God grant me the serenity
To accept the things I cannot change;
Courage to change the things I can; and
Wisdom to know the difference.

Living one day at a time;
Enjoying one moment at a time;
Accepting hardship as the pathway to peace;
Taking, as He did, this sinful world as it is,
    not as I would have it;

Trusting that He will make all things right
If I surrender to His Will; that
I may be reasonably happy in this life and
Supremely happy with Him forever in the next. Amen.

READING OF THE 12 STEPS WITH RELATED SCRIPTURE

A volunteer uses a laminated copy of the Steps* to lead the crowd to repeat in unison each Step, then the volunteer reads the Scripture alone. Words are on the projection screen. For variety, we alternate between the standard version and a version Pastor John developed which uses "Therefore" Scriptures* — everyone says "Therefore," loudly, together before the volunteer continues alone with the rest of the Scripture verse.

TWO WORSHIP SONGS

The band leads us in two praise and worship songs. The words are up on the screen.

HOLY COMMUNION

We serve communion at every service. A seasoned Serenitarian oversees communion, inviting everyone to take part and explaining how we take Holy Communion.

> The first person will break off a piece of bread and give it to you saying, "This is His body broken for you."

> The next person will extend the cup and say, "This is His blood shed for you." You then dip your bread into the juice and eat it.

The leader then calls forward those who will be serving and calls up to the microphone the volunteer scheduled to share **What Communion Means to Me** (3 - 5 minute time limit). While the volunteer is sharing, servers are off to the side sanitizing their hands. Then the volunteer who shared joins the one overseeing communion to serve the juice to those who will be serving the attendees. The servers take their positions across the front and we hear the joyful news, "**The table is open!**"

We have had anywhere from two to four pairs of servers. When we find the service is running too long we add another station to receive communion. When we have a special event we add another station. If attendance is low for some reason, we can decrease the number of stations.

CHILDREN DISMISSED TO CLASS

We ask parents to sign up their children for class on their way into church, indicating whether or not they are staying for Overcomers

* Available from www.SerenityChurch.net > PDF downloads

and including a cell phone number in case a teacher needs to text them during the service.

Teachers and children gather outside the sanctuary when they are done with communion. Teachers pick up the sign-in sheets and, after comparing the sign-in sheet with the children gathered and making sure they have everyone, the teachers lead their group to the classroom.

Worship Song

During communion and while teachers and children are gathering, the No Regrets Praise Band plays and sings a quiet song. Song lyrics are on the screen. At the close of communion, the band leads worshipers in the rest of that song or an additional song before they leaving the stage to take communion, themselves, from a pair of servers waiting for them at the bottom of the steps.

Pastor John takes the stage in his bare feet. (God, from the burning bush, instructed Moses to remove his shoes because he was on holy ground. This practice began, unplanned, at the first-ever worship service of Serenity Church when Jeff Scott looked down after preaching and realized, with embarrassment, he had stepped out of his flip-flops. No embarrassment needed! It was the start of a tradition which reminds the preacher he is there to hear and deliver God's message.) The pastor introduces himself in the 12 Step way including how many days he has been sober. He welcomes everyone again in a thorough way and may make announcements at this point before beginning his sermon.

Announcements are still a problem for us at Serenity Church. Most folks do not read them in the bulletin and do not notice them in the slides running on the screen before church starts. Most folks cannot hear them unless they are delivered in a serious, attention-getting manner. Most attenders are sitting in their fear or pain and need to be jogged out of it in order to hear announcements. We use any and all means.

Provide What Is Needed

Pastor John instructs his "lovely assistants" to come forward with their baskets of supplies—needed items such as Bibles, bulletins, and pens; these are handed out to those lacking them. He explains that if someone takes a Bible we have no expectation of getting it back, and he encourages them to pass it on during the week ahead to someone who does not have one.

Sermon: Bulletin and PowerPoint

Pastor John delivers his sermon utilizing both an outline in the bulletin and a PowerPoint presentation on the screen behind him. He constantly draws listeners back into his message by saying, "Write this down!" to fill in blanks in the message outline.

The screen displays the phrase with blanks, just like in their bulletin. As he delivers the phrase, it is filled in on the screen with the word they should write down.

Some Scripture passages and quotations from *The Big Book of Alcoholics Anonymous* also appear on the screen at appropriate times. Page numbers for each passage are mentioned by Pastor John, provided on the screen and in the bulletin.

Good News: At some point in his sermon Pastor John mentions his promise to "...never finish a sermon without giving you some good news. Write this down. ... Now if that isn't good news, I don't know what is!"

You may be thinking all these ways of getting the truths of Scripture through to those assembled may be, as has been said, "putting the cookies on the lowest shelf." At Serenity Church, we are not offering cookies. Cookies are not life sustaining. We are offering meat! God sacrificed His only Son. We use these methods because we are speaking to people in pain.

- We use these methods to overcome the gospel they were raised on or ran away from which was not a pure gospel but had the conditions of works added.

- We use these methods because we are speaking to people who think the Good News is for other people, not for them.

- We use these methods to keep on telling them the truth: There is *nothing* you could, should, or would do to *earn* salvation or anything else from God.

Yeah, you're unworthy, but you're still welcome!

Everyone is unworthy, standing naked and alone; but the truth is we are not naked, and we are not alone! The blood of Jesus covers us. His clothes of righteousness cover us. And these clothes come with His presence.

To listen to a Serenity Church Sermon on the Serenity Church App, choose Message (the microphone icon) then pick a series, then a message. Or visit the website www.serenitychurch.net.

Offering

We pass baskets (one per row) to collect an offering and white slips. White slips are a quarter-sheet of paper pre-printed to collect personal information on one side and prayer requests on the other. A place is also provided so folks can request a call to encourage them in their recovery. This information is then passed on to a seasoned Serenitarian and 12 Stepper. Prayer requests are sent via e-mail to those who have signed up to be Serenity Prayer Warriors.

Prayer and Worship

While the No Regrets Praise Band leads in two or three additional worship songs, folks have an opportunity to pray with each other or with a pastor or seasoned Serenitarian stationed around the edge of the room. We try to have at least one person of each gender available for prayer. We also have added low stools or pillows so folks can come forward to humble themselves before the Lord and pour their hearts out to Him.

Since we obeyed the Lord in this way, offering a humble place of prayer without any seasoned Serenitarians in the way, many good things have happened in the lives of individuals and in the church as a whole. Now that our folks have gotten used to bringing their requests to the Lord on their knees, we have had to offer more kneeling locations because a line was forming!

The 12 Promises and The Lord's Prayer

After the last song, a volunteer reads the 12 Promises* from a laminated copy while the words are on the projection screen for everyone to see. Then the volunteer leads us in praying The Lord's Prayer by using a segue such as,

> Let this family represent what we can do together that all of us failed to do alone, with Whose help?

In the early days The Lord's Prayer was followed by the Overcomers song (see next page).

* Available from www.SerenityChurch.net > PDF downloads

OVERCOMERS

Everyone is invited to take a 10 minute break before gathering for a meeting of the Overcomers. Our middle school and high school age kids gather together with a pair of seasoned Serenitarians for some on-site, age appropriate activity. Children remain in class with their teachers who move from their lesson to crafts and games.

CLEAN UP

Since we meet in rented facilities that will be used by the host church within a few short hours, we do our best to clean up after ourselves before the janitors arrive.

Overcomers Song

When Serenity Church first began, we sang the following song every week—until we were kinda sick of it! We only sing it from time to time now, but it was a great way to remind ourselves of why we were doing what we were doing, and it helped draw folks together from every type of recovery group.

To listen to a sample audio, find it in the Serenity Church App. Choose Music > *Take My Hand* album > Song 10.

Overcomers
Jason Kelley, 2006

VERSE:

In the beginning
We were powerless,
But then we decided to turn our will and lives before our God.
Why does Satan try to torment us?
Doesn't he know that we are free because of Jesus?

CHORUS:

We are overcomers, overcomers,
We're jumping over every obstacle that gets in our way.
We are overcomers, overcomers,
We have serenity cause of the promise He made.
We are overcomers, overcomers,
He has wiped our slates clean, so we're no longer ashamed.
We are overcomers, overcomers
We have everlasting life cause of the price that He paid.
Hey, hey!! (3x)

VERSE:

It doesn't matter
How low we've gone.
People will see through our suffering how loving is our God.
Why does Satan try to torment us?
Doesn't he know that we are free because of Jesus?

What Can Happen from Doing What We Do

CARDBOARD TESTIMONIES

Provide a large piece of posterboard or card board and markers. On Side 1, have each person answer the question: What was my life like before? On Side 2: What is my life like today?

Have everyone line up with their posterboard and, while gentle music plays, each one takes a turn walking to the middle of the front, lifting their board showing Side 1, wait 10 - 15 seconds then flip to Side 2, wait another 10 - 15 seconds, then walk off.

This activity allows folks to assess, to see the progress in their journey; it also helps folks get to know each other better and, above all, it glorifies God.

Here are some of our Cardboard Testimonies

Side 1: Trying to Keep Another from Wrecking Their Life Was Really
          Wrecking Mine
Side 2: Serenity (The Absence of Mental Stress or Anxiety)

Side 1: He Took a Cold Stony Heart of Judgment
Side 2: Replaced it with a Compassionate Heart of Grace Ez. 36:26

Side 1: In the Gutter
Side 2: On My Knees

Side 1: Full of Fear, Resentment, and Anger
Side 2: Comfort, Calm, and Content

Side 1: Caterpillar
Side 2: Butterfly

Side 1: Addicted to Anything That Changed How I Felt
Side 2: Clean, Sober, and Grateful to Feel 7,625 Days!

Side 1: Sinful Musician
Side 2: No Regrets Praise Band through Christ!

Side 1: I Used to Think I Did Not Have Anything to Overcome
Side 2: With God's Help I Am Overcoming Things Left and Right!!

Side 1: In the Pit All Alone with a Shovel Digging for a New Bottom!
Side 2: On Top of the Mountain with Jesus!!

Side 1: Lost, Hurt, Lonely, Angry, Selfish, Violent Drunk, Hurt Others, Abandoned God and Faith
Side 2: Asked for Help, Found a Spiritual Way of Life, Renewed Hope, Jesus Is My Higher Power, Reborn

Side 1: Him: Porn Addict and Pothead
Side 1: Her: Didn't Believe Love Was for Me
Side 2: Him: 10 Months into a Relationship with Her, 4 Months Clean, Sober, and Happy
Side 2: Her: We're Getting Married!

Side 1: Drunk and Suicidal
Side 2: I Am Alive by God's Grace

Side 1: Crippled by FEAR and Beer
Side 2: Healed by FAITH

Side 1: Control Issues, Self Righteous, Low Self Esteem, Lacking a God of My Own Understanding
Side 2: Less Controlling, Full of God's Righteousness and Love, God Controls My Life

Side 1: Broken, Lost, Lonely, Discouraged, Depressed, Hurt by Church
Side 2: Loved, Full, Comforted, Amazed, Light, Healed by Church

Side 1: Pregnant Teen, Drug Addict, Depression, Isolation, Too Dependent on Others, Low Self Esteem
Side 2: Clean Today, Better Mom, Wife, and Nurse, Happy Through Jesus

Side 1: Lost My Lonely Pride
Side 2: Gained Eternity with Him

Side 1: Selfish, Self-centered, Lost, Insecure, Drugs, Ashamed, Self-pity
Side 2: Miracle, Picked up and Loved, Healed in Every Way

Side 1: Hopeless and Helpless
Side 2: Loved and Accepted

Side 1: Anger, Controlling, Rage, Manipulation, Self-centered
Side 2: Peace, Love, Joy, Patience, Kindness …

Side 1: Atheist
Side 2: Believing More than Ever!!!!

Side 1: Drug and Alcohol Abuse, Promiscuous, Needy, Enabler,
        Liar, Control Freak, Anger Outbursts
Side 2: Responsible, Consistent, Dependable, No Longer Depressed,
        Al-Anon and Overcomer

Side 1: Life Was about Me—Selfish, Lost, Lonely, Rages, Not the
        Mother I Wanted to Be, a Rehab Woman, Self Destructive
Side 2: Free, Restored to Him, Forgiven, Attentive Mother, Giving,
        No More Self-inflicted Harm, I Am His

Side 1: Empty and Alone
Side 2: Never Alone Again

Side 1: I Didn't Realize I Had a Choice
Side 2: Thank You Father and the 12 Steps of AA, I Do Have a
        Choice

Side 1: Drugs, Sex, and Porn Addict, Self-centered, Mad, Mean,
        Angry, Liar
Side 2: I'm an Overcomer, Great Child of God, Happy, Glad, Great,
        Wonderful

Side 1: Drugs, Cutting, Cigarettes, Depression
Side 2: I Have Better Ways to Cope with Stress, Depression, and Pain

Side 1: I Have 4 Children Waiting for Me in Heaven but—
Side 2: —I Have 4 Beautiful Children Here!

Side 1: Pain, Alone, Afraid, Depressed, Lost or Dead, Silence,
        Downward Spiral No Help, No Word from God, No Light,
        No Hope
Side 2: God Is All Love over Us All, Christ Pushed Away the
        Darkness, I'm under His Care

Side 1: Alcoholic, Addict, Adulterer
Side 2: Through Christ, a new man—Eph 4:24

Side 1: Food Addiction, Family Rejection, Alcohol Addiction
Side 2: In Him I am helped. I'm Healthy, Loved, and Sober—Ps. 28:7

> The LORD is my strength and my shield;
>   my heart trusted in Him, and I am helped:
>   therefore my heart greatly rejoiceth;
>   and with my song will I praise Him (Psalm 28:7 KJV).

TESTIMONY: PRAY WITHOUT CEASING
Mac Martin

If we think about prayer the same as we do the breath in our lungs and the blood from our hearts, we think rightly. Our blood is always flowing and our breathing never stops. If it does we get weak and sometimes we die. We are not conscious of this going on, but it always is; it never stops. We are not conscious of Jesus keeping us tuned in to God. But if we are obeying Him this is what He does. Prayer is not an exercise, it is life.

One time my aortic valve became clogged and was about the size of a pin head. My blood stopped flowing and my organs began to shut down. My lungs could not get rid of the fluids and my breathing was becoming more difficult. I became unconscious on the way to the hospital in an ambulance. And I do not remember going through the doors of the hospital, and I did not remember anything for six days. I could not pray for myself, but others prayed for me.

I use this analogy because prayer flowing through us constantly is just as important as the blood flowing through our veins or the air flowing through our lungs. Our blood, and the air we breathe, sustain our bodies. But prayer is food for the Spirit. Remember this when you are in the dark and when things start getting tough. If you have not been praying constantly and you need help, you may be calling on a malnourished spirit that is as weak as you are to help you out of your bind.

This is even more important to those of us who are in recovery. We not only have to provide nourishment for our spirits but we also have to build up the spirit of those we are helping until they learn to provide their own nourishment. When we stop praying, we get weak. And when our enemy surrounds us, we cannot fight back. We have to pray a whole lot in order to build up the strength of our spirit, and protect ourselves, which we could have done a lot faster and easier had we already been praying constantly.

Those doctors fixed my heart so my blood could flow again. My lungs started working well and I could breathe again. Jesus taught me how to pray by using the Lord's Prayer.

Paul sums it up in 1 Thessalonians 5:16-22:

> Rejoice always, pray continually, give thanks in all circumstances; for this is God's will for you in Christ Jesus. Do not quench the

Spirit. Do not treat prophecies with contempt but test them all; hold on to what is good, reject every kind of evil.

Jesus said,

Whatsoever ye shall ask of the Father in My name He will give it unto you (KJV).

The Big Book of Alcoholics Anonymous says:

We are not cured of alcoholism [or what harms us]. What we really have is a daily reprieve contingent on the maintenance of our spiritual condition. ... Every day is a day when we must carry the vision of God's will into all of our activities. ... How can I best serve Thee—Thy will [not mine] be done. These are thoughts which must go with us constantly. We can exercise our will power along this line all we wish. It is the proper use of the will.

If we practice this without ceasing, we will develop a vital sixth sense and become God-conscious.

Testimony: The Secret of the Serenity Prayer
Linda Widhalm, September 26, 2009

Thou wilt keep him in perfect peace, whose mind is stayed on Thee: because he trusteth in Thee (Isaiah 26:3 KJV).

It was a Saturday, September 2, 2006, a few minutes after noon. We were in the den and my husband, Pat, was reading aloud to me. When the phone rang, I glanced down at the caller ID, took a deep breath, looked at my husband, and said, "I think this is the call we've been waiting for." The caller ID read: **** Co Sheriff.

During the six months before the phone call, I had been crying out to the Lord and waiting on the Lord to show me when and how I was to have any influence in my son's life. He had begun drinking regularly with his friends and to excess since the day he turned 21. He was choosing not to heed what he had been taught at school, at home, and at church about alcohol. He ignored warnings about drinking with minors. We had told him if he ended up in jail, he should not call to be bailed out until he was ready to submit to whatever we asked of him. Then the prayer-filled time of waiting began.

Now, suddenly it seemed, the waiting was over. I breathed a prayer for God to help me and answered the phone.

Seven hours later we all three drove into the parking lot of Serenity Church and took our seats together as the opening song was underway. I say "our seats" because Pat and I had regularly attended Serenity Church on Saturday nights since it began three months before. It is a good thing Serenity Church has a "come as you are" policy. Staying overnight in jail can be rather aromatic!

My son had promised to give us 90 days, so for three months he had no contact with friends. No phone. No computer. No answering the door. Eventually we let him work on a job with his brother-in-law. He pretty much went where we went and hung out with who we hung out with. We started hanging out at AA meetings and Overcomers meetings! Overcomers is a fellowship of men and women who have been affected either directly or indirectly by something destructive that is out of our control.

Serenity Church, Overcomers, and AA meetings all have several things in common, but today I want to share with you the first one: The Serenity Prayer. You might be saying to yourself, I have known that prayer forever, seen it on mugs and almost everywhere else I look.

But there is a secret to the Serenity Prayer.

Every 12 Step meeting begins with the Serenity Prayer. Since Serenity Church began, I had been reciting the Serenity Prayer every Saturday night at about 7:05 p.m., but from the moment I sat with my son in that first Overcomers meeting I began *praying* the prayer.

To welcome me, they gave me this little coin that has the Serenity Prayer engraved on the back. After waiting all those months for my chance to have an influence in my son's life, I sure did not want to blow it. I knew I needed help, too. From the first minute I stepped into the room I knew I was there for me, no matter what happened in my son's life.

So I carried the coin in my pocket. I even made clothing choices so I was sure to have a pocket. When something disturbing came up, I slipped my hand in my pocket and held onto the coin, reminding myself I was facing life and its issues differently now. I began praying that prayer just about every time I felt any feeling of any sort. Anxiety—God grant me the serenity. Fear—God grant me the serenity. Sadness, anger, hurt—

> God grant me the serenity to accept the things I cannot change, courage to change the things I can, and wisdom to know the difference.

Applying that little prayer to each circumstance relieved me of so many unfounded emotions, which, in turn, halted unwanted actions. Having a proper response myself kept me from taking responsibility for the actions of others. My eyes were opened to how much I was manipulated by others. I even began quoting the prayer to others when they were sucked into other people's business and trying to suck me in with them.

One day I rewrote the prayer: God, grant me the serenity to accept the things that are none of my business, courage to change the things that *are* my business, and the wisdom to know the difference.

Someone shared in an Overcomers meeting another version of the prayer: God, grant me the serenity to accept the people I cannot change, courage to change the one I can, and the wisdom to know it's me.

So, the Secret of the Serenity Prayer is to actually pray it. Then listen to that still small voice. Whenever the enemy rushes in with those overwhelming feelings, I just beat him off with the Serenity Prayer because God will keep *me* in perfect peace when my mind is stayed on Him, because I trust Him (Isaiah 26:3).

The Serenity Church Prayer
by John Featherston

Jesus is Lord. Jesus is Lord. Jesus is Lord.
Jesus is Lord. Jesus is Lord.
Father, please show us what we're missing.
Father, please give us what we're missing.
Heal our minds, our hearts and our bodies—
Through Christ.
This is our prayer. Jesus is Lord.

See to it that no one misses the grace of God
(Hebrews 12:15a).

Acknowledgments

My special thanks to my husband of 40 years, Pat, for the many meals prepared and other essential tasks done so I could stay focused on getting the book done. I could not get by without your encouragement and help. Thank you.

My special thanks to the rest of my family for your encouragement, contributions, and other help along the way. Jessica and Jason, Breila and Nathan, Lisa and Joel, Jeremy, Mom, Elaine and Don. Thanks to my grandchildren, Emily and Mercy, who made contributions to the book. To my many other grandchildren, who love me and provide a welcome break with their smiles, laughter, and hugs.

Special thanks to my Sereni-family for showing me a better way to live and how to apply the truths of Scripture in a practical, life-changing way. Thank you for your contributions to the book, and for loving me.

Special thanks to my friends, John and Kay Featherston, David and Trena Hunt, and Jason and Jessica Kelley, for allowing me to serve alongside you in this great adventure; also for proofing text, making contributions, and that you'll "Always Be There."

Special thanks to Christine Hunt. God brought us together again at just the right time to get this book published. It would not have happened without your guidance, hard work, and special talents. Thank you.

Special thanks to my son, Jeremy, for the cover photography, and to him and John Featherston for their willingness to share with us their very appropriate arm art.

The Jesus in you all is Light. He takes all the broken pieces we yield to Him and, together, makes a remarkable, beautiful kaleidoscope of redemption and life.

Index

175